# Making Instruction Work

or *Skillbloomers*

## Robert F. Mager

*The book for every instructor*
*who prepares others*
*for the world of work.*

**Lake Publishing Company**
Belmont, California

BOOKS BY ROBERT F. MAGER

Preparing Instructional Objectives, *Revised Second Edition*

Measuring Instructional Results, *Second Edition*

Analyzing Performance Problems, *Second Edition*
(with Peter Pipe)

Goal Analysis, *Second Edition*

Developing Attitude Toward Learning, *Second Edition*

Making Instruction Work

Developing Vocational Instruction
(with Kenneth Beach)

Troubleshooting the Troubleshooting Course

Library of Congress Catalog Card Number: 87-82497
Printed in the United States of America

1.9  8  7  6  5  4

# Contents

# Kneedimples

## (A Magerfable)

Once upon a time in the land of Upsyde Downs, the Keeper of the Wisdom said to the next in line, "Doodly, you are soon to become of age, so it is time for you to enter the world and learn to Trip the Light Fantastic. It is time for you to become the best that you can."

So Doodly hurried off with his heart in his hand and a spring in his step, for he was truly eager to become all that he could.

When he finally arrived at what he believed to be the Greatest Learnatorium in all of Upsyde Downs, he was ushered to an audience with the Keeper of the Knowing.

"You have truly come to the right place," intoned the Keeper. "We have all of the Knowing there is to Know. So if you will learn what you are told, you will surely become all that you can."

Doodly was mightily impressed. He was sure he had found the Right Place. After all, didn't they have Starbright Projectors and Redeye Comblabulators with shimmering screens? Of course they did! Weren't the instructors the greatest stars of the Light Fantastic? Of course, they were! So, convinced of the soundness of his choice, Doodly applied himself in earnest. He listened keenly and wrote down what he heard. He put a mark beside all the right answers, and wrote the most masterly essays. Inevitably, he rose to the top of the class, because there simply wasn't anything about Tripping the Light Fantastic that Doodly couldn't tell you about.

Finally the appointed day burst over the horizon. Doodly was handed his three-dimensional holographic diploma, along with as much pomp as could be arranged under the circumstances. He was so proud that he showed it to everyone in sight. But when at last the oohs and aahs abated, he tucked his diploma under his arm and went off to find . . . a Position. Naturally, he went first to Upsyde Fantasies, the most magnificent theater in all of Downs.

"Here is my diploma," he said proudly to the Keeper of the Entertainment. "I am ready to Trip the Light Fantastic and show that I have become the best that I can."

"Well, well, well," said the Keeper, with a lift of his eyebrows. "Anyone with a diploma as shiny as yours certainly deserves respect. And as we happen to have an opening for tonight's performance, you're hired."

So within hours it came to pass that Doodly faced his first Opening Night. He was so excited that his synapses literally twanged in anticipation. Then, just as he was giving his shoes a final sparkle, he heard the fanfare and the great clashing of cymbals—his cue for his first Grand Entrance. And he rushed onto the Stage of Life.

But the Glorious Triumph was not to be. For hardly had he approached the center of the stage before he got all tangled up in his own feet and fell flat on his face. Kersplat!

"Oh, my," said Doodly to the sweet young partner twiddling on her toes and trying to swallow a horrendously loud giggle. "They certainly taught me the tripping part of it, but I wonder what happened to the Light Fantastic? I could do *this* well before I started."

And wonder he might. Because try as he did, and he did try, all he could ever manage was a very ungainly but hilarious squat that caused everyone to roar with laughter whenever he walked upon the stage.

And from that day on, whenever people heard that Doodly was on the program, they would come from miles and miles and miles around to watch. Oh, not to watch him Trip the Light Fantastic, of course, because he hadn't actually been taught how to *do* that. If truth be told, they came to watch Doodly squat.

And the moral of this fable is that . . .

*SKILL DOES NOT BLOOM FROM WORDS ALONE.*

Or, in somewhat less poetic terms, telling isn't the same as teaching. Though it is a remarkable accomplishment to have developed the skills and knowledge needed to be considered competent in one's craft, those skills are not the same as those needed for teaching that craft. Just as an ability to *make* a tuba is not the same as an ability to *play* one, an ability to *play* one is not the same as an ability to *teach* someone else to do likewise.

Therefore, those who would like to share their competence with others will take steps to learn the skills by which that end is accomplished.

ROBERT F. MAGER

*Carefree, Arizona*
*May, 1987*

# 1 || Introduction

## WHAT IT'S ABOUT

The world of instruction has changed from the days when instruction followed the lecture-in-the-morning–lab-in-the-afternoon approach and the only tools in the instructor's tool kit were the lecture, the lab, and on-the-job training (OJT). It has changed from the days when instructors were selected because they were good at their specialty, whether or not they knew anything about communicating that specialty to others. It has changed from the days when instructors were allowed to teach as much about a subject as time would allow, regardless of the relevance of the content to the need of the individual student.

Now, there is a craft of instruction almost as sophisticated as your own specialty. It is a craft rich in procedures and techniques for assuring that students develop important skills and rich in practices that will send them away with a desire to apply what they have learned and with an eagerness to learn more.

This book is about that craft. It isn't about *all* the bits and pieces of the craft. It's only about those pieces that will ensure that (a) instruction is the correct solution to a problem, (b) the objectives of the instruction are derived from demonstrated needs, (c) the substance of the instruction is adjusted to what each student needs, and (d) instructional practices contribute to, rather than detract from, student eagerness to learn more. It's about how to make instruction work as well as possible with the tools at hand.

Those are major accomplishments. Fortunately, they are within the grasp of those with even the most limited of instructional resources—they need no special approval or budget to make them work. The tools are at hand and available to all.

## WHO IT'S FOR

This book is for those vitally important people who prepare others for the world of work. It is for the indispensable instructors of technical and vocational courses who strive to provide their students with marketable skills—for those who teach so that others may achieve economic independence and self-respect in their own worlds.

## WHAT IT'S FOR

The purpose of this book, therefore, is to describe and illustrate those components of the instructional craft that are of particular use to those who teach critical skills to others. But just as there are far more words in the English language than you will ever need or use, there is far more to know about the craft of instruction than you can, or need, put to practical use. This book is about those practical pieces—the pieces that will make your instruction lean, on target, motivating, and effective.

And there is another purpose. People who prepare others for the world of work are often treated like second-class citizens by their more academic neighbors. Looked down on as though their efforts were trivial, rather than of critical importance, these instructors often are required to sit in the back of the academic bus. Too often they are the recipients of the hand-me-downs: the most decrepit buildings and the oldest equipment and academically oriented texts. So another goal of this book is to shape instructional information directly for those who teach others to perform job-related tasks—to speak in plain language whenever possible and to define terms when it is not, and to offer concrete examples to illustrate the procedures being described.

Though the chapters of this book cannot send you away highly skilled in the procedures being described, they will point you to those procedures that, if applied, will increase the elegance of your efforts.

> **NOTE:** If you find yourself thinking that it is impossible to apply any of the techniques described in this book because you are "stuck with the 50-minute hour" and there's nothing you can do about it, or because you "just don't have the time," skip ahead to the last chapter, "Course Improvement." Skim the chapter and then apply the "Course Improvement Checklist" *to the course you are teaching or are preparing to teach.*

> **ANOTHER NOTE:** Many instructors are literally dropped into a course, given a textbook, and instructed to "Go teach." Though this situation may not be ideal from either the instructor's or student's point of view, it often cannot be avoided. Even though in this circumstance, you have to "hit the ground running," you can still apply—immediately—some of the course improvement procedures described in this book.

# 2 | Strategy of Instructional Development

There is only one justification for instruction: it is that one or more people cannot yet do something *and* there is a need for them to be able to do it. Unless these two conditions exist, there is no excuse for instruction. Put the other way around, there is a valid reason for instruction only when there is a need for people to (1) know how to do something they (2) do not yet know how to do.

That may sound like a trivial idea, until you consider the amount of time you've spent in classes thinking or saying, "But I already *know* that," or "I don't *need* to know that." Such thoughts indicate the waste of instructional resources caused by thoughtless insistence on instructional ritual when no sound reason exists for it.

One of our goals as instructors is to impose ourselves as little as possible on the lives of others. Just as the ethical physician's goal is to treat only those in need of treatment and only for as long as the need lasts, our goal is to instruct as effectively and as efficiently as possible only for as long as the need exists, that is, until each student can perform as desired.

And because we are humane and because our job is to help people to *grow,* our intent during instruction is not to hurt, belittle, humiliate, insult, or otherwise demean our students. In other words, our first primary intention is to *do no harm.*

5

To accomplish these intents, we deliberately avoid engaging in instruction when none is needed and carefully avoid acts or procedures that will cause students to shrivel . . . either in skill, self-confidence, or spirit. We deliberately seek out procedures and practices that will give our students the skills they need, as well as the motivation to use them and to learn to perform them better.

## INSTRUCTIONAL STRATEGY

The strategy (that is, the grand plan) for accomplishing the above intents therefore includes actions and procedures by which one can

1. determine that there is a need for instruction;
2. describe what the instruction should accomplish, deriving these objectives from the world in which the student will be expected to function;
3. determine which of these objectives students have already accomplished;
4. develop, try out, and revise instruction that will fill the gap between what students can already do and what they need to be able to do;
5. implement the instruction;
6. find out how well it worked; and
7. improve it.

That's the overall strategy. The tactics (procedures and techniques) used to put the strategy into practice, however, depend on who you are, where you are, and on the current state of your instructional practices. Instructors will find it practical to select those sets of items from the supermarket of instructional practices that are most appropriate to their circumstances.

## THE WORLD OF HUMAN PERFORMANCE

Before venturing into specifics, I'd like to offer some perspective into the larger world of human performance.

### Instructional Technology

When we set out to help people to do something that they cannot now do yet need to do, we dip into a bag of procedures currently referred to as "instructional technology." These are the techniques and procedures by which we influence what people *can do*. When there is a skill or knowledge deficiency to be eliminated, one dips into this bag and selects one or more remedies to solve the problem. (Terminology note: Though the current rubric is "instructional technology," you can substitute "craft of instruction." Both refer to state-of-the-art practices: the best practices currently available through which to modify human capabilities.) Figure 2.1 lists some of these practices.

*Figure 2.1*

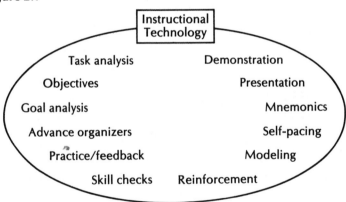

**Mission: To change performance capability.**

## Performance Technology

The craft of instruction, however, is a subset of a larger collection of procedures and techniques known as "performance technology." When people *already know how* to perform but are *not* performing as desired, instruction won't help. Such situations call for application of a different set of tools, techniques aimed at modifying the "do do" rather than the "can do." These tools encourage people to do what they already know how to do. For example, if students already know how to study but don't, more instruction on study skills won't help. Instead, what is called for is the application of strategies that will increase the likelihood that they will do what they already know how to do. Some of these strategies are identified in Figure 2.2.

**Figure 2.2**

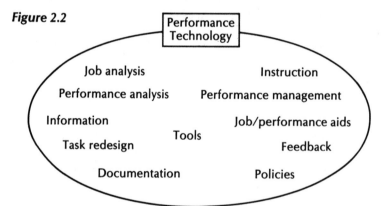

**Mission: To facilitate desired performance.**

As you are well aware, people often don't do what they know how to do because of one or more of the following reasons:

- They don't have the tools to perform as desired.
- They aren't given the authority to perform as desired.
- They don't know what they are expected to do.
- They are punished for performing as desired.

In these instances remedies other than instruction are called for, such as

- information (manuals, policies, notices, etc.)
- performance (job) aids
- feedback for present performance
- performance management (arranging the environment so that desired performance is allowed and rewarded, rather than punished)
- tools
- authority to perform as desired
- task redesign (to simplify the desired performance)

The point is that instruction is useful only for stimulating desired performance when people do not yet know how to perform the expected way.

## Management

Both the instructional and performance technologies are subsets of an even larger domain referred to as "management." Management involves the allocation and control of available resources toward the accomplishment of goals and objectives. No matter whether we are talking about the management of a giant corporation or about management of a ship, a church, a family, a classroom, or our own personal lives, we are talking about allocating and controlling available resources to accomplish goals and objectives. Some of these resources are shown in Figure 2.3.

**Figure 2.3**

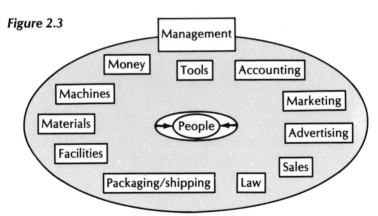

**Mission: Allocate and control resources
to accomplish goals and objectives.**

Any corporation, for example, has a variety of resources available with which to accomplish its goals: machinery, money, production procedures, research information, blue-printing technology, marketing, advertising, law, accounting practices, and so on.

One of the key resources is people. It takes people to do many of the things that need doing. To get things done in a way that helps rather than hinders the accomplishment of the goals, however, people have to do things in a productive rather than an unproductive way. The function of the performance technology is to make that happen. It reaches for the tools of that technology when people already know how to perform and reaches for instruction when they don't.

*Figure 2.4*

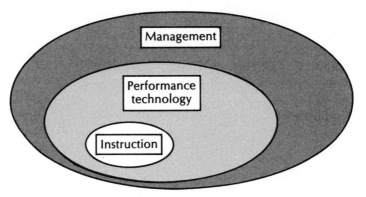

# 3 | Instructional Components

This chapter is an overview of the main instructional technology procedures and techniques and one key procedure from performance technology. The chapters that follow describe how each procedure fits into the larger scheme of things, describe how to do it, and offer one or more examples. Though some of the procedures may be new to you, the overall strategy will be familiar, simply because it asks you to do to your instruction what you already do in your own craft: decide what you want to accomplish, apply tools and techniques to accomplish it, and then determine how well you did.

> NOTE: Procedures are described in this book in the approximate order followed when a full instructional development project is undertaken. But it is neither necessary to apply them in the order shown nor to use *all* of them. In truth, *any one* of them can be used in the improvement of your instruction. You don't have to eat all the candy in the box to enjoy the sweetness of a bite or two.

The components of the instructional process fall into four broad phases: analysis, development, implementation, and improvement. Though the fourth phase is not technically part of development or implementation, it is important to the continued success of the instructional enterprise.

1. *Analysis:* Derive the key outcomes of the instruction.
2. *Development:* Develop, try out, and revise the instruction.
3. *Implementation:* Conduct the course.
4. *Improvement:* Check the results and make adjustments.

**Figure 3.1**

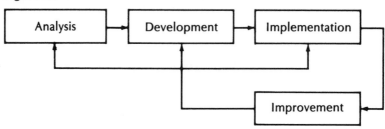

Each of these phases includes a number of steps or procedures, some of which will be more important to you than others. Though quite a number of procedures and practices are available by which one can maximize instructional elegance, only some will be applicable in your own environment. For example, those working in the vocational school environment will probably have fewer occasions to use the procedure called "performance analysis" than those working in organizations where instruction is but one means to a larger end.

## ANALYSIS PHASE

The moral of one of my fables says that if you don't know where you're going, you might wind up someplace else—and not even know it. That seems pretty obvious. But how can you decide where to go in the first place? How can you decide on a worthy destination?

The analysis procedures available to the instructional developer are intended to deal precisely with these issues. They help to answer questions such as these:

- Is instruction called for in this situation?
- What is worth teaching?
- Who is the target audience for this instruction?

- What should this instruction accomplish?
- What does competent performance look like?

The answers to these questions make it easy to prepare instruction that will teach people the things that will add value to the individual student and to avoid teaching things that won't.

There are other reasons to take the time to apply the procedures described in Part I of this book, one of which leads to increased satisfaction in the teaching process itself. Once you have identified the important outcomes your instruction should accomplish, regardless of whether those outcomes were derived by your own analysis or someone else's, you as an instructor are in a position to use your best wisdom and experience in the achievement of those outcomes. Once the intended outcomes are known, you can use your best judgment about how to help each student to competence, rather than feel compelled to use a cookie-cutter approach that imprints the same instruction onto everyone.

As a rule of thumb, tell yourself that no matter how much or how little development time is available to you, you can productively spend up to half that time answering the questions listed above.

Analysis is the key to instructional elegance.

## Performance Analysis (Chapter 4)

Though it often seems hard to believe, instructors are frequently asked to build courses to teach people what they already know or to use instruction to solve problems that can't be solved by instruction.

The performance analysis helps to prevent these instructional errors by revealing the differences between what people are actually doing and what they should be doing, by detecting which of those differences can be eliminated by instruction, and by pointing to solutions that will help solve the problem. Though this procedure isn't often used by those in the vocational-technical environment, it is an important tool in the arsenal of those more interested in results than in ritual.

## Task Analysis (Chapter 5)

The task analysis (sometimes referred to as a job/task analysis) results in a step-by-step description of what a skilled person does when performing a relatively sequential task, regardless of whether the steps of the task are mainly cognitive (mental) or psychomotor (physical). It is a way of making competent performance visible, much as a blueprint provides a way to make the components of a finished product visible. With a task analysis it is easy to determine the skills that must be in place before the entire task can be practiced by a learner. In this way it is possible to make sure that all important skills and knowledge are taught.

## Goal Analysis (Chapter 6)

The goal analysis is useful in revealing the important components of performances usually described in abstract terms. Thus, a goal analysis is called for when it isn't easy to say what students should be able to do when performing competently.

If, for example, students will be expected to be "personable," a goal analysis will reveal exactly what a person would have to *do* to be worthy of that label. Instruction can then be offered to teach those components of the desired "doing" that the students don't already know.

## Target Population Description (Chapter 7)

This tool consists of a description of the key characteristics of those who will be the recipients (the targets, the audience) of the instruction. By knowing their characteristics, it is possible to better mold the instruction to each student: to select objectives, examples, terminology, and procedures that will best allow each student to accomplish as desired. It is one of the key techniques for making instruction work.

## Course Objectives (Chapter 8)

These are statements that describe the key outcomes desired from the instruction. They are derived from the analysis procedures described above to ensure that the instruction is focused on what students should be able to do to become functional on the job. Objectives describe instructional targets, much as blueprints describe manufacturing targets.

### Skill Hierarchies (Chapter 9)

Skill hierarchies are simple diagrams showing the dependency relationships between the skills of the course. They are useful in determining which skills *must* be learned before others should be attempted. They are also useful in solving problems caused when the equipment available for student practice is limited.

### Course Prerequisites (Chapter 10)

Prerequisites describe what students must be able to do before they can profit from your instruction. Prerequisites are derived from the *assumptions* made about what students are able to do when they enter your course and from decisions about what will and will not be included as course content.

## DEVELOPMENT PHASE

The development phase includes the drafting of measuring instruments (tests), as well as development and tryout of the instruction itself. Though some consider one or more of these steps to be part of the analysis phase, it is a hair unworthy of splitting.

### Criterion Tests (Chapter 11)

Also referred to as "performance checks" or "skill checks," these are the instruments by which students and instructors determine whether the instruction works, that is, whether a student can perform as an objective demands. They are the instruments by which students and instructors alike can determine whether the student is ready to move to the next unit of instruction. They are not intended to determine how well a student performed in comparison with other students.

### Relevant Practice (Chapter 12)

Derived for each objective, this is a description of what must be provided if students are to practice the substance of the objective. The description lists tools and equipment needed, as well as environmental requirements. It also lists any other persons that may be required for practice to occur under realistic conditions. Since practice is essential to skill development, it is important that the practice be crafted correctly.

### Content Derivation (Chapter 13)

With objectives, criterion tests, and relevant practice and audience descriptions in hand, instructional content can be derived to facilitate accomplishment of each objective. The procedure ensures that students will learn what they need to know, while not having to attend to irrelevant content and things they already know.

### Delivery System Selection (Chapter 14)

This procedure determines the combination of media, resources, and other things that will be most useful in delivery of the instruction. It identifies the means by which learners will be taught what they need to know *before* they can practice, and it identifies the things that will be needed to provide the practice itself. Media decisions are simple to make and take little time.

### Module Development (Chapter 15)

Modules (lessons, instruction units) are drafted according to a "floor plan" that assures (a) practice in the objective of the module and (b) feedback regarding quality of the practice. It also includes the knowledge that must be learned before a student can profitably practice the objective. Performance-based rather than time-based, a module includes the instruction needed to accomplish a given objective, rather than that which will fill a unit of instructional time. If the previous steps have been completed (which is easier than it looks at this point), the instruction will practically write itself.

## Sequencing (Chapter 16)

Modules (instructional units, lessons) are sequenced to (a) maintain and enhance student motivation, (b) build new or complex skills onto existing ones, and (c) provide periodic practice of things already learned.

## Tryout (Chapter 17)

A key step in instructional development, the tryout provides information about whether the instruction is working and about where improvements need to be made. Those who are serious about instructional quality will always insist on at least one tryout before putting a course "on line." Instructors who must do their own development should always consider their first on-line run-through as a tryout.

# IMPLEMENTATION PHASE

Implementation means getting the instruction to the student. Implementation at the state of the art means instructing in a way that will help students learn what they don't already know, as efficiently and as humanely as possible. As most instructors work under somewhat less than ideal conditions, compromises have to be made. Implementation, therefore, means instructing in a way that applies the state of the art as well as the situation will allow.

## Course Procedures (Chapter 18)

Course procedures are derived from ideal characteristics and local constraints. These are written down so they may be given to the students. A course map is prepared showing students how the course modules are related to one another.

## Implementing the Instruction (Chapter 19)

Materials are collected, the environment is arranged, and the course is then ready for delivery.

The instruction is then made available to the students. For each module students review the objective and decide whether they need instruction or practice before attempting to demonstrate their competence. If so, they work through the instruction, practice until they feel ready, and then complete the criterion test for that unit or module. If they meet or exceed the criteria, they advance to the next unit. If not, the instructor diagnoses the weakness and prescribes a remedy.

## IMPROVEMENT PHASE

Because vocations change, because new techniques and devices become available, and because the characteristics of incoming students change, professional instructors take steps to keep their instruction up-to-date. They do this mainly by following steps that answer these key questions:

1. Does the instruction work (do what it's supposed to do)?
2. Is it of value (to the students and the organization)?
3. Is it up to date (uses best available instructional techniques)?

## SUMMARY

Instruction is designed to fill a need. Objectives are derived from the requirements of the job itself, the instruction is developed and implemented to accomplish those objectives, and steps are taken to find out whether the instruction succeeded as intended.

The chapters that follow describe each of the procedures named above, and provide an assortment of examples. Though the descriptions are offered in the approximate order in which they are usually accomplished, it should not be implied that any step is completed and then forgotten. Instructional development always involves modification of earlier steps in light of what develops later.

The systematic development of instruction is not specific to any subject matter or vocation. Regardless of the intent of the instruction, the procedure for its development is basically the same.

A final word before proceeding. Though the content of this book must be presented in some sort of order, you should not believe that you can reap benefits only by applying all of the techniques, and in the order presented. This is not the case. It isn't true. Don't you believe it. Your instruction can be improved by the application of almost any one of these procedures, whether or not others are applied as well. The final chapter will suggest a priority for improvement of instruction already in existence—a sort of "bang-for-the-buck" list that will provide clues about what might be the most productive next step.

# PART

# I

# Deriving the Outcomes

# 4 | Performance Analysis

**Situation:** *Someone has suggested that you either create a course, modify an existing course, or locate and purchase a course. The request comes from someone who, for some reason, is dissatisfied with the current performance of a group of people or who feels that a course will solve a problem. You want to find out whether instruction is really indicated in this situation, and if not, what solution is indicated.*

*Or you have noted that one or more of your students aren't doing what you want them to do, that is, that there is a difference between their actual and desired performance. You want to know what you can do about it.*

Suppose someone came to you and said: "Look. These students aren't coming to school on time. I want you to develop a course to fix that." What would you teach? The history of time? How to read clocks? The importance of promptness? Pendulum appreciation? You see the point. Students already know how to get to school on time. If they don't do it, it is because of some other reason. If there is a solution to the problem, it has to be something other than instruction.

Like a hammer, instruction is only one tool for getting a job done. It is the tool of choice when students cannot now do something they need to be able to do. It is the tool to reach for when capabilities need to be expanded. But what about those instances in which students already know how to do what they need to know? Or part of what they need to know? What to do when people can already perform as desired but aren't doing it for reasons having nothing to do with skill? What about the times you say to yourself, "I want my students to feel free to ask questions when they don't understand, but they don't." Or what about the times you note other differences between what they are and should be doing? Clearly, a technique is needed for sorting solutions to match problems. Enter the performance analysis.

The performance analysis is used to suggest the proper course of action in those instances where people aren't doing what they should be doing. It is a way to find out whether the differences between what they're doing and should be doing can be eliminated by instruction or whether some other action is called for. This procedure is needed mainly by those who are expected to develop instruction *at the request of other people*. It is needed—desperately—by all instructors who are told:

- "We need a course."
- "Improve their motivation."
- "Fix their attitude."
- "They don't understand the fundamentals."
- "We have a training problem."

Unfortunately, many administrators and managers don't know how to analyze problems having to do with people performance. So when they see a symptom—someone doing something they shouldn't, or not doing something they should—they jump to the conclusion that the person *doesn't know how* to do it. So they run to their instructors to request some training. In thousands of instances, that training is then used to "teach" people things they already know. A total waste. If only a small amount of time (often a few minutes will do) had been taken to find out why people weren't performing to expectations, a proper—and less expensive—remedy could have been selected. Hence the importance of the performance analysis.

To make sure that instruction is used only when it will teach people what they don't already know, we need to know

a. what they are now doing, and
b. what they should be doing.

If there is a difference, then we need to determine whether the difference is due to a skill deficiency or to something else. If they aren't doing what they should be doing because they don't know how, then instruction may be the correct remedy. But if they already know how and aren't doing it, then something else will be the remedy.

## HOW TO DO IT

The performance analysis is intended to

a. identify discrepancies between what people are now doing and what they should be doing,
b. determine whether the discrepancies are due to lack of skill or to something else, and
c. suggest a remedy or remedies that will reduce or eliminate the discrepancies.

Here's a brief description of the steps in this procedure.

1. Name the category (job title) of the person or people whose performance is being questioned.
2. Describe as specifically as possible what it is they are doing that causes someone to say there is a problem.
3. Describe specifically what it is they should be doing.
4. Determine the "cost" of the discrepancy by estimating what it is costing in such things as aggravation, frustration, turnover, scrap, insurance rates, time lost, money lost, equipment damage, customers lost or good will damaged, accidents, and so on.
5. If the estimated cost of the discrepancy is small, stop. In other words, if it's only a problem because you say it is, and it isn't having any impact on the rest of the world, stop.
6. If the cost is great enough to warrant going on, determine whether the target people know how to do what is

expected of them. Answer the question, Could they do it if their very lives depended on it?

7. If they could, then they already know how. Now determine why they aren't doing what they already know how to do. This is done by determining the consequences and obstacles to performing.

   a. What happens *to the performers* if they do it right?
   b. What happens *to them* if they do it wrong?
   c. What are the obstacles to performing as desired?

8. If they couldn't do it, answer these questions:

   a. Can the task be simplified to the point where they *could* do it?
   b. Did they *ever* know how to do it? (If so, they only need practice.)
   c. Is the skill used often? (If they do it often and still don't do it right, they need feedback. If they don't do it often, and they used to know how, they need a job aid, such as a checklist or a piece of sheet music.)
   d. Do they have the potential to learn to do it? (If not, they should be transferred or terminated.)

9. The answers to these questions lead to the drafting of potential solutions. These solutions must address the problems exposed during the analysis. For example, if it is discovered that people aren't performing because they don't have the authority to perform as desired, then one part of the solution must propose a way to remove that obstacle.

10. Once potential remedies are drafted, determine how much it will cost to implement each remedy.

11. Compare the cost of the solutions to the cost of the problem.

12. Select one or more solutions that are (a) less expensive than the problem itself and (b) practical to apply.

   Figure 5.4 shows these steps in a flowchart.

A performance analysis usually takes only a few minutes to complete. When it takes longer, it is only because time is needed to locate the information with which to answer one or more of the questions.

**Example:**   To show you that this analysis is easy to do once you've gotten the hang of it (i.e., practiced it half a dozen times), here's an example of how it might be done "live." In this example an instructor who teaches computer repair in a technical school is approached by the dean.

*Dean:*   We need to beef up your course on trouble-shooting.

*Inst:*   I'm certainly willing to do that. What seems to be missing?

*Dean:*   Well, I've had calls from a couple of companies who are complaining that their troubleshooters won't use the hotline when they're supposed to.

*Inst:*   What do you mean?

*Dean:*   If they can't clear up a problem within 22 minutes, they're supposed to call the hotline and talk to the "hotshot" about it. But they don't.

*Inst:*   What do they want me to do about it?

*Dean:*   They think you should beef up your course.

*Inst:*   Don't they know how to use the telephone?

*Dean:*   Of course they do.

*Inst:*   Do they know the procedure for calling the hotline?

*Dean:*   Of course they do. But they don't.

*Inst:*   So they already know how to do what they're supposed to do. Instruction isn't going to help. Would it be OK for me to talk to a couple of their troubleshooters?

*Dean:*   I don't see why not.
   *(Two days later.)*

*Inst:*   Dean, I think I've got a handle on this problem.

*Dean:*   What did you find out?

*Inst:*   Well, if the troubleshooter calls the hotline he's likely to get some verbal abuse—sarcasm—from the hotshot on the line.

*Dean:*   That would hardly encourage anyone to call in a second time.

*Inst:*   There's more. If the hotline is called, and then the troubleshooter fixes the problem alone, the hotline gets credit for the fix.

*Dean:*   Good grief.

*Inst:*   There's even more. Troubleshooters are expected to stay on the problem until it's fixed. That means they get overtime pay if it takes them longer.

*Dean:*   Some system.

*Inst:*   Yep. This is another instance where performers are being soundly punished for doing the very thing they're expected to do and rewarded by overtime for doing what they aren't supposed to do.

*Dean:*   No wonder they don't do what they're supposed to do—and know how to do. What do you suggest?

*Inst:*   I suggest you talk with the managers who brought this up, and gently ask them the questions that will make it clear to them that company policy is getting in the way of desired performance. I'd suggest you try to lead them to see that the solution to this problem isn't instruction, but a change in the way performers are treated when they do what's expected of them.

As pointed out earlier, knowledge of the performance analysis procedure is needed by those who develop instruction at the request of other people, which means that it is important for vocational and technical instructors and essential for developers working in the industrial environment.

**To Learn More:**   See Resources #1 and #7.

# 5 || Task Analysis

Situation: *You have determined that there are things that students should be able to do that they cannot now do, and you want to determine what is worth teaching. This will be accomplished, in part, by deriving the important outcomes of the instruction from the tasks to be learned. The first step is to determine the components of competent performance.*

One of our goals is to develop and deliver instruction that prepares people to perform in a useful manner in a "real world" situation, whether that "real world" happens to be a job or another course. Another goal is to make sure that the instruction itself teaches those useful skills with as little wasted motion and effort as possible. To accomplish those goals, we need to know what the job or craft consists of and what peole have to know before they can begin practicing the tasks of the job. Enter the task analysis.

Task analysis is the name given to a collection of techniques used to help make the components of competent performance visible. It is a set of ways to draw a picture of what competent people actually do, or should do, when performing a task. From this picture it is then possible to derive what *others* would have to be taught so that they also can perform competently. It is a way of visualizing the steps in a procedure, the key decisions that are made while performing the procedure, and how to tell when to begin and end the procedure.

There are several ways to go about a task analysis. Some of the approaches break desired performances into microscopic detail, and others only into moderate detail. In practice, one uses the procedure that provides the level of detail needed to get the job done, that is, the level that will make the analysis serve its purpose. That means using the analysis procedure that will best answer the questions, What do competent people do when performing this task? and What would *anyone* have to know before he or she could begin practicing this entire task?

As I said, there are several ways to carry out a task analysis. To use a method that is more complicated or "sophisticated" than needed to get the job done is either wasting time or showing off. The procedures described below will be useful in most of the situations you will encounter.

## WHAT'S A TASK?

A *task* is a series of steps leading to a meaningful outcome. There. That's the standard definition, but it's only helpful once you know what it means. Think of it this way: Every job is made up of a collection of tasks, things that you do during the course of a month that you refer to as "my job." (Note that these tasks are not necessarily related, that your job does not necessarily consist of a *coherent* set of tasks. For example, you may find yourself answering the telephone one minute, filling out a form the next, and dictating a letter the next. These are tasks that are all part of the job, but are not related to one another.) These tasks have a beginning, a middle, and an end. You are referring to a task whenever you ask someone to "Go and _____ ": take out the garbage, tie off an artery, change a tire, set a bone, interview a prospective employee, write a report, make a verbal report, cut a head of hair, do a preflight check, adjust your computer drive speed, and so on. Each of these tasks has a beginning and an end, with a series of steps in between.

A *step* in a task, on the other hand, would be something like tighten a nut, pick up a scalpel, select a component, ask a question, press RETURN, enter name in box 3, remove the cover, or take a deep breath. Each represents *one* of the actions that need to be taken in order to reach the meaningful outcome. Here are some other examples of one step in each of several tasks.

| Task | Step in the task |
|------|------------------|
| Disassemble a device | Disconnect power |
| Make a dress | Pin pattern to fabric |
| Pick a lock | Select picks |
| Cash a check | Verify endorsement |
| Apply at bank for loan | Grovel |

## WHO SHOULD DO IT?

Who should carry out the task analysis? That's easy. If there isn't anyone else to do it, and if it hasn't already been done, then you're elected. Fortunately, that doesn't mean you'll be saddled with an impossible or time-consuming chore. In fact, you may find it rather enjoyable. All you need to do is locate and observe a competent performer (who may be yourself).

"Wait a minnit," I hear you shouting. "I can't spend time going to where people are performing the job or profession I'm teaching. Besides, I don't teach the entire curriculum. My students don't go directly to the job; they go to other courses."

Good point, and I understand your predicament. Folks in industry have no trouble deriving their instruction from observation of competent performers (at least the well-trained analysts don't). Those analysts are able to follow the procedures that allow them to say, "Aha. This is what we want people to do on this job; these are the things they don't yet know how to do; and so these are the things we will have to teach them." They can even say, "Now that we've derived outcomes, you teach this clump of objectives and I'll teach that clump."

Those teaching in vocational and technical school environments, however, are working in a "cottage industry" environment where each instructor is in business for himself or herself, where each instructor decides what to teach and how much of the subject to include in the time allotted, where five instructors teaching a course with the same name are likely to be teaching five different courses, where the objectives of one course in a series are not derived from the prerequisites of the next one in line, and where the objectives of the last course in line are not derived from the job itself.

But all is not lost. You can use yourself as one source of information for the task analysis. Then again, you must know some people who do this thing in the "real world." You can talk to them. And you can find out from the instructors of the next courses in the sequence what they expect students to be able to do when they enter those courses. Their prerequisites are your objectives. Your main goal should be to prepare students for the world they will find themselves in when they leave you.

## HOW TO DO IT

The task analysis consists of (a) drafting a task list (an activity sometimes referred to as job analysis), and then (b) describing the steps in each of the tasks listed.

### Task Listing

The first thing to do is to make a list of all the tasks that make up the job. It makes no difference that one task may be considered critical and another trivial. They are all to be listed, so that a complete snapshot of the job can be studied. If those performing the job are expected to perform the task, write it down. You will decide later which of them will need to be learned and whether you will be the one to teach them.

For example, every job involves some sort of paper work. People are expected to complete forms, write reports, read job tickets, fill out requisitions, write letters, and so on. If paper work is expected, those tasks should be included on your list. Many jobs also require people to interact with other people. Sometimes it is with customers, sometimes with patients or victims, sometimes with superiors, or with colleagues. Appliance repair people are expected to "instruct customers" on how to avoid certain problems in the future. Managers are expected to "conduct exit interviews," and police officers are expected to "interview witnesses." Whatever its nature, if the competent job performer is expected to do it, add it to your list.

**Example:** Electronic Technician.

1. Troubleshoots to locate troubles.
2. Clears troubles from equipment.
3. Completes parts requisition forms.
4. Reads schematic and/or wiring diagrams.
5. Uses test equipment.
6. Calibrates test equipment.
7. Interprets test results.
8. Records test data.
9. Uses soldering equipment.
10. Applies first-aid procedures.
11. Cleans and sharpens tools.
12. Cleans work area.
13. Uses hand tools.
14. Disassembles equipment.
15. Assembles equipment.
16. Interacts with customers.

Notice that each of the items on this list begins with a verb, a "doing" word. This is one way to tell whether the item being described is a task or just a piece of subject matter. For example, if an item reads "anatomy" or "measurement," you would know instantly that subject matter is being described rather than a task.

## Task Detailing

The second step in the analysis is to list the steps and decisions involved in performing each of the tasks on the list. For each task, answer these questions:

1. When is the task performed (what triggers initiation of the task)?
2. How is the task performed (what are the steps followed and decisions made while performing the task)?
3. How would you know when you're done (when the task has been satisfactorily completed)?

**List.**

There are two practical ways to list steps and decisions. One is simply to begin listing them on a piece of paper, as you would build a shopping list. Here are two examples.

**Example #1:**   Task: Start an IV.

*When initiated?*   a. When patient's chart says to do it.

1. Read patient's chart.
2. If IV is not called for, stop.
3. If IV is called for, collect equipment.
4. Get material to be administered.
5. Locate patient.
6. Verify that correct patient has been located.
7. Prepare patient psychologically for the procedure.
8. Sterilize site where needle is to be inserted.
9. Locate vein.
   . . . and so on.

*When completed?*   When IV is running according to requirements.

**Example #2:**   Task: Clean spark plugs.

*When initiated?*   a. When plugs are dirty.
                    b. When customer asks.

1. Open hood.
2. Locate spark plugs.
3. Cover fender with protective material.
4. Remove plugs.
5. If plugs are cracked or worn out, replace them.
6. Clean the plugs.
7. Check gap in each plug.
8. Adjust gap as necessary.
9. Test the plugs.
10. Replace plugs.
11. Connect ignition wires to appropriate plugs.
12. Check engine performance.
13. If OK, go to step 15.
14. If not OK, take designated steps.
15. Clean tools and equipment.
16. Clean any grease from car.
17. Complete required paper work.

*When completed?*   When engine runs smoothly.

Even though these were examples of relatively simple tasks, you will note that there were decisions to be made and that it is somewhat awkward to show in a list just how the actions resulting from those decisions should be handled.

## Flowchart

There is a better way to show the steps and decisions involved in performing a task. It is called flowcharting. A flowchart is easy to read and clearly shows the alternatives to be followed when decisions are involved. Furthermore, it reveals where information is still missing.

To flowchart a task, you need only two symbols to depict the steps of the task: a rectangle to depict actions and a diamond to depict decisions. Other shapes, such as ovals and squares, may be used to depict various outcomes, but the rectangle and the diamond are all that are needed to show the components of the task itself.

**Figure 5.1**

Begin by writing down the event that causes the task to be performed. For example:

- Phone rings.
- Customer asks _____ .
- Red light comes on.
- Grinding sound is heard.
- Screen shows error message.
- Patient screams.

Then write down what happens next. If the thing that happens next is an action, write it in a rectangle. If it is a decision, write it in a diamond, and draw lines coming *out* of the diamond to the different things that people would do as a result of the decision. Often there are only two alternatives: do thing A if the decision is yes, and do thing B if the answer is no.

For example, if I were to flowchart the spark plug cleaning example, it would look like this:

**Figure 5.2**

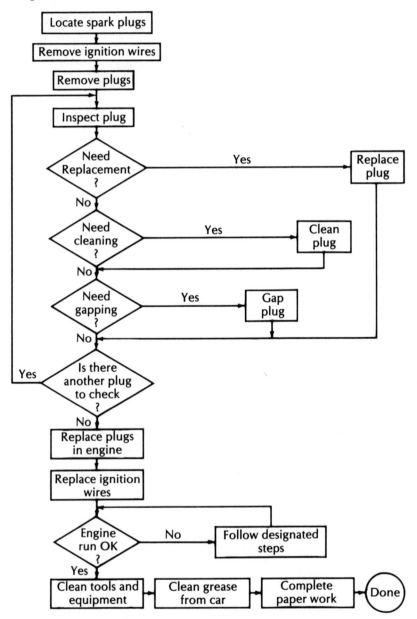

**NOTES:**

    a. Do not include instruction in the analysis. Remember that the purpose of the analysis is to visualize what competent performance looks like so that better decisions can be made about how to get more of it. Putting "how to learn it" comments in the task analysis puts the cart before the horse and defeats the purpose of the analysis.

    b. Statements such as "Select a screwdriver" are not considered decision points and so do not belong in a diamond, because no matter which screwdriver is selected, the action that follows the selecting action is the same. Use a decision symbol only when one decision would lead you to a different *action* than would another decision.

    c. Don't be concerned if one part of your analysis seems to be more detailed than another. The purpose of this exercise isn't to produce some tidy document for display; the purpose is to help answer the question, "What would *anybody* have to be able to do before practicing this entire task? When the analysis is detailed enough to answer that question *for each step*, consider it finished.

    d. The quality of the analysis is unrelated to the straightness of your lines. So don't waste time with a ruler. Do your flowcharting on a large piece of paper, and do it with a pencil.

Notice that flowcharts make it easy to see where key decisions have to be made. It is also easy to see what actions should follow those decisions.

**Example #1:**   Here is a flowchart that shows the key actions followed by someone troubleshooting equipment at the customer's location.

*Figure 5.3*

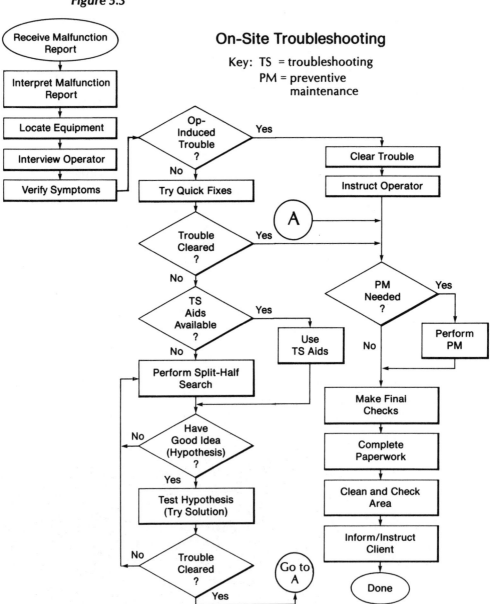

**Example #2:** This flowchart shows the steps followed in a performance analysis and is useful in both school and industrial environments.

*Figure 5.4*

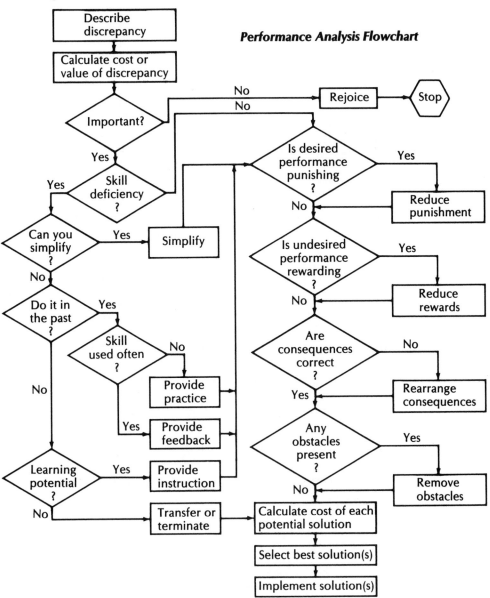

**Example #3:**   Here is a flowchart showing the key steps in the process of conducting a task analysis when the information has to be retrieved (squeezed) from a subject matter specialist.

*Figure 5.5*

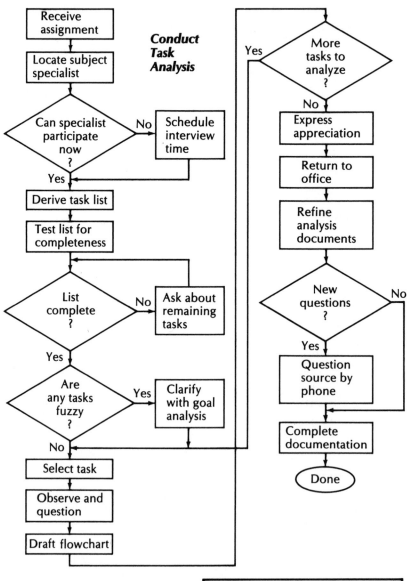

Courtesy of Mager Associates, Inc.

**Where We Are.** We're considering procedures that will help us derive content for our instruction so that we can guarantee that content to be job-related and can be assured that the instruction will fill a real need. We are considering sources of information from which to derive our instructional objectives.

## DERIVING SKILLS

Once the task analysis shows the components of competent performance, you can derive the skills that *anyone* would need before practicing the entire task. To do this you need to forget about students for the moment. You'll think a great deal about them later. At this point you are not interested in any particular person; you are interested only in naming the skills that *anyone in the world* would have to have before practicing the task step you are considering.

## HOW TO DO IT

1. Consider each step of your analysis in turn.
2. Beside the step write the skills that anyone would have to have before they could practice *that step*.
   *Note:* Lots of steps won't require you to write anything beside them because they are so simple or trivial, such as, "Pick up wrench," or "Locate Box 3." Don't make it harder than it is.
3. When you have finished, delete the duplications from your list of skills. For example, it is likely that you have written "Read English" beside several of the steps because, among other things, someone would have to be able to read to perform that step.
4. The skills remaining are those about which you will draft objectives when you get to that step.

**Example:** The example below shows the skills that would be required to perform *three of the steps* in the troubleshooting task shown earlier. Note that these skills have nothing to do with particular individuals. *Anyone* would have to have these skills before being able to practice that step in the task.

**Figure 5.6**

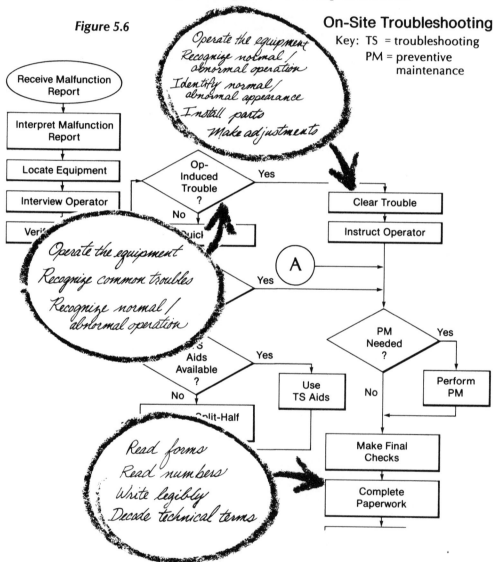

**On-Site Troubleshooting**

Key: TS = troubleshooting
PM = preventive
maintenance

Receive Malfunction Report

Interpret Malfunction Report

Locate Equipment

Interview Operator

Veri...

*Operate the equipment*
*Recognize normal /*
*    abnormal operation*
*Identify normal /*
*    abnormal appearance*
*Install parts*
*    Make adjustments*

*Operate the equipment*
*Recognize common troubles*
*Recognize normal /*
*    abnormal operation*

Op-Induced Trouble?

Yes

No

Clear Trouble

Instruct Operator

(A)

Yes

... Aids Available?

Yes

No

Use TS Aids

Split-Half

PM Needed?

Yes

No

Perform PM

*Read forms*
*Read numbers*
*Write legibly*
*Decode technical terms*

Make Final Checks

Complete Paperwork

**To Learn More:** See Resource #12.

# 6 | Goal Analysis

**Situation:** *You are deriving the important outcomes of your instruction and have run into some abstract expectations, such as "They should be motivated," or "They should be more safety-conscious." You want to know how to handle those abstractions and you want to know what, if anything, you need to teach in order to better accomplish those goals.*

Suppose that you have been carrying out a task analysis. You have been identifying the tasks that make up a job, and you have been drafting flowcharts depicting what competent performers do, or should do, when performing each task. You then show this work to someone in the craft whose opinion you value, or to a colleague, or to a dean, or to a client, who says: "This is great. This is just what these people are supposed to do." And then adds, "But we also want them to be conscientious about their work and more thorough in their reporting. And it's important that they be professional." Since you can't watch people conscientiousing, or thoroughing, or professionaling, what to do?

The fact is that not everything we want people to be able to do can be described in terms of tasks—not everything can be directly observed. Sometimes, rather than being expected to carry out tasks, people are expected to exhibit certain characteristics or states. For example, you may decide, or be told, that students should

- be motivated
- demonstrate courtesy to _____
- be safety-conscious
- value total patient health

- have good analytical ability
- be problem-solvers
- be self-starters
- exhibit good leadership characteristics

or any of hundreds of other possible states. When expectations are stated as "fuzzies"—vague terms—a task analysis won't help. Since there is no task to watch anyone perform (you can't watch people leadershipping, or attituding), a different tool is needed.

So when you or someone else says that one or more of these abstract states are important to achieve, that's the time to reach for the goal analysis procedure. Goal analysis will help you to extract the meaning (if any exists) from the abstract words so that you will (a) know what performances students would need to exhibit when demonstrating their achievement of the goal and (b) know what you should do to accomplish the goal. In other words, the goal analysis will show you how to get more safety consciousness, or good grooming, or self-starting, or more of any goal you want to achieve.

Notice that I slipped in the word *goal* to refer to the abstract states we're talking about. I also referred to those abstractions as fuzzies. That was deliberate. A goal is a broad, or general, intent; an objective is a specific target. Unless you can tell one when you see one, you're talking about goals rather than about objectives. The purpose of the goal analysis is to determine what it would take in the way of human performance to be able to say that the goal has been accomplished. The purpose is to say what someone would have to *do* to be considered "safety-conscious" or "competent"—to say what someone would have to do to be worthy of being labeled with the goal.

## WHEN TO DO IT

The goal analysis procedure is used whenever you have questions like these to answer:

How can I help them to understand?
What do they mean by "fundamentals"?

How can I tell if they're motivated?
How can I teach them to be competent?
How can I teach them to be diligent?
What do I do about the affective domain?

The goal analysis is used because someone says there is an abstract state or condition that is important to do something about and because nobody will tell you how to recognize accomplishment of that state or condition. The goal analysis will help you know how to "recognize one when you see one."

## HOW TO DO IT

There are five steps to the procedure. The steps are repeated as needed.

1. Write down the goal, using whatever abstract terms express your intent. Be sure your statement is described in terms of outcomes rather than process. For example, make it say, "*Have* a favorable attitude toward _____ ," rather than "*Develop* a favorable attitude toward _____." That will help keep you out of the trap of thinking about *how* you are going to accomplish the goal before you know what the end result should look like. In other words, it will help keep you from fussing around with bows and arrows before you've constructed the target.

2. Think about what would be happening if the goal were achieved. Think in terms of people performance. What would people have to do or say, or refrain from doing or saying, before you would be willing to say that they represent the goal? List as many performances as you can think of.

3. Sort the list. Many of the items you listed will be as fuzzy as the one you started with. That's okay. Just take each fuzzy that doesn't yet say something about performance (something you can see someone do or hear someone say), write it on another piece of paper, and follow steps 1 and 2.

Continue until you have a list of performances that collectively represent the goal. Continue until you can say, "Yes. If someone did these things and refrained from doing these other things, I would say they represent the goal," or until you can say, "Yes, I can count whether these things are happening or not happening."

4. Expand the words and phrases on your list into complete sentences that tell when or how often the performance is expected to occur. This will help you to place limits around the expected performances. It will help to say "how much" performance will satisfy you (or someone else). For example, a goal analysis on security-consciousness included the item "no unattended documents." When expanded into a complete sentence it read, "Employee always locks sensitive documents in safe before leaving the room."

   This step will also help you to weed out statements that on second thought don't say what you mean.

5. Test for completeness. Review the performances on your list (there will usually be from one to seven items and only occasionally more), and ask yourself, "If someone did these things, would I be willing to say that he or she is _____ (goal) _____ ?" If so, you are finished with the analysis. If not, return to step 2 and add the missing performances.

**Example #1:**   A shop instructor I once knew completed a task list describing the tasks he wanted his students to be able to perform when they left his course. But he was uneasy about the list.

"There's something missing," he said. "There's more to it than just these tasks."

"Oh," I said. "Can you give me an example?"

"Sure," he replied. "I want them to be safety-conscious."

"That sounds reasonable." I said. "Can you tell me how to recognize a safety-conscious person when you see one?" And we were off into a goal analysis. Not long after, we had a list of "performances" (step 2) that included these items:

- Understands the need for safety practices
- Wears hard hat in designated areas
- Sweeps shavings from work area
- Wears safety goggles while performing designated tasks
- Uses saw guard on table saw
- Appreciates safety equipment

"How can you tell when someone understands the need for safety practices?" I then asked.

"Well, they follow the safety rules" was the reply. So we deleted that fuzzy and replaced it with "Follows safety rules."

"How can you recognize someone who appreciates safety equipment?" I asked next.

"Easy," he said. "They take good care of it." So we deleted the second fuzzy and replaced it with a performance. Our list then looked like this:

- Follows safety rules
- Wears hard hat in designated areas
- Sweeps shavings from work area
- Wears safety goggles while performing designated tasks
- Uses saw guard on table saw
- Keeps safety equipment in good working condition

Since we could count whether these items were or were not happening, we moved on to the fourth step. When we were done, our items looked like this:

1. Follows all posted safety rules whenever in the shop.
2. Wears hard hat each time a designated area is entered.
3. Keeps lathe area clean by sweeping shavings into the bin provided.
4. Wears safety goggles while performing the tasks posted.
5. Does not remove saw guard without permission while using table saw.
6. Keeps personal safety equipment in good working condition.
7. Reports faulty shop safety equipment.

*Your* definition of safety-consciousness would be different, of course, because your situation and environment are different. But that doesn't matter. What matters is that you describe what it would take for the goal to be accomplished. Only then will you know what action to take to accomplish it.

The final step was simple. When my friend said, "Yes, if people did those things on the list I'd be willing to say they were safety-conscious," we were done with the analysis.

**Example #2:** While I was working with the training staff of an automobile manufacturer, it became clear to me that one company goal was to improve customer service over the coming year.

"No," the training director said after thinking about it, "What we want to do is to provide quality service."

"Where?" I asked.

"In auto service" was the reply. It was important to determine just what part of the business he was talking about, because the definition of "provide quality service" would be different in the bookkeeping department than in auto service.

After working through the first four steps described above, we had a list of performances that looked like this:

- Customer complaints are written down.
- Service reps refrain from arguing with customers.
- Service reps smile when talking with customers.
- Service reps listen carefully (i.e., do not have to ask customers to repeat things they have already said).
- Repaired autos are ready when promised.
- Repaired autos are not returned to customers with dirt or grease either inside or outside the car.
- Causes for the complaints have actually been remedied.
- There is less than 1 percent return (cars returned because the repair was not properly completed).

"If these things happened," I then asked, "Would you be willing to say that you were providing quality service?"

"Wel-ll-l," was the cautious reply, "I guess so. But we want to provide the quality service without the mechanics using up more parts than they need."

"I can understand that. But does number of spares used have anything to do with how you would recognize quality service?"

"I guess not directly. But it's important."

"Tell you what. Let's focus on quality service until we're sure we can recognize it when we see it, and then we'll move on to the other issue."

Which we did.

**Example #3:**  The following flowchart was developed as a result of a goal analysis. An instructor was asked to develop instruction that would teach students to use "good judgment" when deciding which criterion level to assign to each (military) task to be taught. She saw immediately that it would be impossible to decide what, if anything, to teach until she knew what "good judgment" consisted of. After the goal analysis was completed, she saw that it would be easy to convert the results into the following flowchart. In effect, the flowchart says that performers will be using good judgment when they follow its steps.

*Figure 6.1*

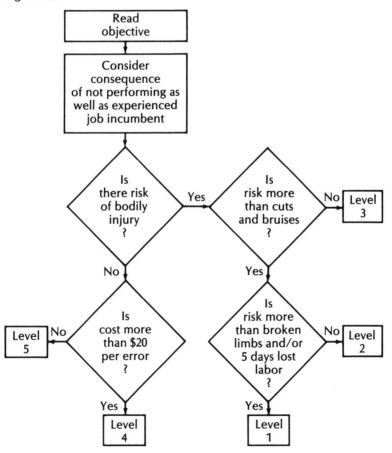

## WHAT TO DO WITH IT

You can see that now that the goal has been analyzed into the performances that represent the goal, it's easy to see what to do next.

1. Put a check beside each of the things that students can already do. If they can already *do* it, you won't get more of it by "teaching" it. If they know how to do it but *aren't* doing it, do a performance analysis to find out why they aren't doing what they know how to do.
2. Consider the items not checked. If they can't do it and need to be able to do it, you or someone else will need to teach them to do it. Decide who will teach what.
3. Complete a task analysis for each of the tasks that must be taught.
4. Write objectives to describe the main outcomes you need to achieve.

*To Learn More:*   See Resource #3.

# 7 | Target Population Description

**Situation:** *You want to develop the information that will help you decide where your instruction should begin and that will help you to better match your instruction to the characteristics of your students.*

No doubt about it: "Target population description" is a piece of jargon right out of the instruction technology bag. But not to worry. It means nothing more than "the students at whom your instruction is aimed." It could be called "audience description," but the word *audience* is generally reserved for a clump of people expecting to be entertained. Since we are not (officially) in the entertainment business, the word *audience* has wrong implications. But as you run into *target population description* below, just keep in mind that it refers to that particular gang of people for whom your instruction is intended, whether they are all alike or all different. So having swept the mystery aside, onward!

To this point we have been considering procedures for deriving the end point, or outcomes, of instruction. With the information derived from the task, goal, and performance analyses, it is possible to write objectives that describe what students should be able to do at the time they leave the instruction. (This is the topic of Chapter 8.) But it will also be extremely useful to think about the "raw material" for the instruction, the students themselves. Just as the objectives will help determine where the instruction should end, the characteristics of the entering students will help determine where the instruction should begin.

Think of it this way: Instruction takes students from where they are to where they need to be, from their present state to a desired state of competence. Thus, the instruction for any individual student should close the gap between the actual and desired competence.

    What they need to be able to do
        (Review your objectives)
    − What they can already do
        (Review your target population description)

= The instruction

The importance of a target population description cannot be overemphasized. Not only will careful thought about your students help determine the starting point of the course, but it will help to shape the course itself. It will help determine which examples are most likely to fit, what vocabulary to use, and even what instructional media and procedures to adopt. For example, if you know your students are active people, you won't make them sit passively for long periods of time. If you know they find reading difficult, you will minimize the reading load by using other ways to present information. If they tend not to be interested in sports, you will avoid examples from that area. If yours is a required course being attended by students who are "kicking and screaming" all the way, you will take steps to insure that students understand the importance of the course and you will take special steps to motivate students to thrust themselves into the activities of the course.

If you spend even a tenth as much time thinking about and describing your students as you do thinking about your subject, you will develop a powerful tool for insuring the effectiveness of your instruction. And you'll find some new ideas for increasing student interest in your subject. "Wait a minute," you may be saying. "Does anybody actually *do* this target population thing?" You bet they do. Look in the folder of any modern instructional developer or instructor and you'll find two to eight pages of prose describing the audience for the intended instruction. And the more diverse that audience, the more detailed the description. There's gold in them thar words (translation: detailed knowledge of the target population is one of the fastest roads to instructional improvement).

Like the other procedures described in this book, the target population description is yet another procedure that you can apply without requiring special permission or changes in policy.

## HOW TO DO IT

1. Begin by reminding yourself that you are going to produce a working document, which will not be published or seen by others. Remind yourself that it is not necessary to organize the content into categories unless that activity helps you to think.
2. Think about the students who will be entering your course, and write down everything you think you know about them. Write the items in whatever order comes to mind. Let one thing remind you of another. If you need help getting started, use these questions as triggers:

   What are their interests?
   Why are they taking this course?
   Do they want to be in this course?
   What is their age range? Sex range?
   What will be the likely male-female split?
   Do they have families?
   What attitudes and biases do you expect them to bring?
   What training and experience have they had in relation to the subject you teach?
   Which of the skills listed on your task analysis do they already have?
   What tools and equipment do they already know how to use?
   What can you say about their physical characteristics?
   What other responsibilities continue during the course (i.e., are they expected to continue doing their job while learning)?
   Are they away from home living in a hotel? How do they feel about their accommodations?

3. Describe the range of a characteristic wherever you can. For example, if you write, "Some will have graduate degrees and some will be new to the subject" or "Some will have 20 years of experience while others will be new hires," you will know immediately that you will have to treat students differently if you are to be helpful to all of them. To treat them all alike would be to bore some and frustrate others, and that's not your goal.

If you are thinking, "But I don't *know* anything about them because I never know who will enroll," you're kidding yourself. You may not know their exact characteristics, but you surely know a lot about the people who *won't* be coming to your course. Will you be teaching kings? Foreigners? Ph.D.'s? Veterans? Opera singers? Come on. Sit down and say what you can about them. And if you really know nothing about them, take a little time to find out. Talk to the registrar. Get some names and call them on the phone. Talk to them. They'll be delighted to tell you about themselves. And they'll be overwhelmed at the thought that an instructor is that concerned.

When you can write two to eight pages that answer the questions on the checklist at the end of this chapter, you can conclude that you know enough about your students to design instruction for them.

## NOTES:

- Describe them as they are, rather than as you wish they were. Write what they can actually do rather than an idealized version of those skills.
- Describe people rather than institutions or policies. Say what people are like rather than what the course will or should be like.
- If you think your students are all different, describe the ways in which they differ. Most of the differences won't have anything to do with how you design instruction. Sure, they're all different. But most of those differences won't matter. Some will matter a lot. You spot the

important differences by asking yourself whether the *same* instructional approach will fit for the *range* of the characteristic you are thinking about. For example, will the same approach work for fatties as well as for skinnies? Sure. But will the same approach (treatment) work for readers as well as non-readers? For active as well as passive people? For experienced as well as inexperienced?

- Don't bother to organize what you write, and don't fret if you say the same thing more than once. Nobody's going to see this document.
- When you have said all you can say, keep the document handy. Add to it as items come to mind (while you're completing other steps in the development process). This is a working document that should grow as you go.

**Example #1:** This example is organized under headings, and the second is more of a mind-dump. Both formats are equally useful.

> T. Pop.: Sales Personnel
> Course: Computer Entry of Orders

### Physical Characteristics

> These people range in age from 25–40.
> About half are male and half female.
> There are no apparent physical limitations.
> Most will be away from home, and the younger ones will be bleary-eyed from too much carousing the night before.

### Formal and Informal Training

> All of the new hires will have at least a master's degree.
> The older reps will have more varied training. Some will have a degree, and others only a year or two of college. They will have 5–20 years of experience with the company.
> All are facile with English, and all are used to writing reports.

All can read quite well.

All are familiar with order-writing; they know company procedures and policies. They just don't know how to enter orders onto a computer terminal.

The younger engineering grads will be familiar with computers; the liberal arts grads will not. Neither will the older reps.

### Anticipated Attitudes

Many of the older reps are apprehensive about this course. They feel they will show up poorly against the younger people who have already used computers. They worry that they are old dogs who won't be able to learn the new tricks.

The older reps will be somewhat resentful about being away from their territory for the duration of the course. They feel they can be making money instead of sitting. Some feel that the computer will make order-writing take longer than it now does.

### Interests

Many students play golf with business colleagues— especially the older males.

The majority are married and have families and spend significant time socializing within the family network.

These people have a lot in common and tend to socialize within the group. Though the older ones are apprehensive about learning to use computers, everyone hates the paper work associated with writing orders.

A few of the recent college graduates have had computer experience and fuss with computers as a hobby.

### Sources of Reinforcement

Many of the older "career" reps just do their jobs to collect a paycheck and receive little self-fulfillment from the job. They know they will never be promoted and no longer want to be. They are very protective of their territory—nobody's going to tell them what to do.

The younger "flow-through" reps are enthusiastic about doing a good job and are pleased with themselves when they know they have done so. They will be promoted and they know it. They are looking forward to the computer automation program. They are not wedded to the existing method and are eager to rid themselves of paper work.

**Example #2:** T. Pop.: Field Service Reps
Course: Appliance Repair

All but about 5 percent are male, and all are married.

They range in age from 25 to 60.

They are all strong enough to do the lifting and bending required by the job. None have handicaps that would get in the way.

They are not diet freaks, though some take regular steps to stay fit.

All have completed high school, and a few have had a little college.

Some have been in the military and received some electronics training there.

Others have learned something of electricity or electronics through home-study courses or while working in dad's shop. Only a few have had appliance training before joining this company.

Their interests include sports (football, bowling, basketball, fishing), TV, gambling, and ham radio.

They don't jog or play tennis, golf, or chess.

They are interested in computers, though many of the older ones are skeptical about their ability to learn much about programming.

They are likely to have mechanically oriented hobbies. These include ham radio, auto or motorcycle repair, and repairs around the house. Obviously they are all mechanically inclined and can handle hand tools with ease.

They are not likely to read for pleasure, though they are not poor readers. They'd rather talk about "the trouble that got away" than read.

They truly enjoy having control of their day. They like to decide how they will spend their time. They would much rather be on the road than in the shop or classroom.

They enjoy receiving customer compliments, and they especially enjoy having a customer ask for them by name because they are pleased with past work. They like to solve customer problems, but some aren't too skilled in customer interaction.

Many like to tell themselves that they will soon start their own business, but few understand the implications of that challenge. They do not like to use test equipment or wiring diagrams in the presence of the customer, because they feel the customer will conclude they don't know what they are doing and that the repair will take a long time. They prefer to wing it rather than use test equipment.

They prefer their training to be "hands-on" rather than theoretical, and they bad-mouth any course that includes as much as 50 percent lecturing. About 20 percent will say they don't know why they've been sent to the course. These either think they are competent enough already, or don't want to learn to handle a wider range of products. These are the reluctant dragons.

NOTE: The descriptions in these two examples contain several clues that should influence the shape of the instruction (content as well as procedures) designed for these populations of students. If you find it hard to spot these cues, try this. Write a brief description of your own personal characteristics and then compare it to the characteristics of any course you've taken. The discrepancies between the way the course was run and the way it should have been conducted to maximize *your* learning reveal things the course developers should have taken into consideration before they developed their course.

## Goofing Off with Questionnaires

Questionnaires are *not* a useful source of information about your students. Why izzat, you may wonder? It's because it takes a great deal of skill and time to prepare a questionnaire that will elicit the type of information you may want. Items have to be drafted, and they absolutely must be tested and then revised, and maybe tested again, before one can have any assurance at all that the questionnaire will work. And people with this specialized skill are rare. If they are skilled in questionnaire development, they are not likely to be working in a training department.

If you just slap a questionnaire together, you aren't going to find out what you want to know, because it's hard to write items that aren't ambiguous. And when faced with ambiguous questions—or questions they think may be dangerous to their job—people will simply tell you what they think you want to hear. What you *will* do is create a great deal of paper work for somebody—reproducing multiple copies, finding addresses in order to mail them, licking the stamps, and so on. You will also create work for someone who has to tabulate the "results." But they will be largely "garbage in—garbage out."

So unless you are looking for a way to expand your empire, consider the questionnaire as an impractical, and largely unworkable, method for finding out about a target population. And don't use a questionnaire just because someone is bedazzled by data gleaned from large samples.

It is far more productive, and faster and cheaper, to talk to a few people directly, either by phone or in person.

## A HELPFUL CHECKLIST

Check your target population description against the following list. Does it include information about:

1. age range,
2. sex distribution,
3. nature and range of educational background,
4. reason(s) for attending the course,
5. attitude(s) about course attendance,
6. biases, prejudices, beliefs,
7. typical hobbies and other spare time activities,
8. interests in life other than hobbies,
9. need-gratifiers (i.e., what would reward them),
10. physical characteristics,
11. reading ability,
12. terminology or topics to be avoided,
13. organizational membership, and
14. specific prerequisite and entry-level skills already learned?

**To Learn More:** See Resources #10 and #13.

# 8 | Course Objectives

**Situation:** *You are prepared to describe what students should be able to do when they leave your instruction so that you will have a sound basis for selecting content procedures and test items and so that your students will have a focus for their efforts.*

To this point the analysis procedures have been oriented toward (a) determining whether instruction is needed and, if so, (b) what the instruction should accomplish. They have been directed at determining just what will be worth teaching. Now it is time to state those outcomes clearly enough to guide you in developing or improving the instruction and evaluation tools and to guide the students about where to direct their efforts. This is not to suggest that you should avoid writing out your objectives until you have completed the analysis steps. Even if you've done no analysis at all, it is still useful to write out what you want students to be able to do when they leave your course.

Statements describing intended instructional outcomes are called objectives because their accomplishment can be measured. *Goals* are broad statements of intent; *objectives* are measurable statements of intent. In plain language, if an outcome statement isn't precise enough to measure whether the outcome has been achieved, it isn't an objective. Because the world grows in wacky ways, objectives have been given many strange names, but whatever its name, an objective is a statement of intended outcome. It describes what you want students to be able to do when they leave your course.

Objectives are a little like blueprints. They provide the guides that will guarantee that you are teaching what needs to be taught. And, because objectives describe *outcomes,* they free developers and instructors alike to use all their ingenuity and creativity in accomplishing those outcomes. Here is an example of an objective to which you can refer as you read the characteristics described below:

*Objective:* Given an accident report and an accident scene, be able to complete the report within 15 minutes.

Criteria: All entered information is correct and legible.

## CHARACTERISTICS OF OBJECTIVES

1. An objective says something about the student. It does not describe the textbook, the instructor, or classroom experiences.
2. An objective describes student performance. It doesn't say anything about what the instructor will do or try to accomplish. It doesn't describe course content.
3. An objective is about ends rather than means. It describes a product of instruction rather than the process of instruction. It describes what students will be able to do when they are competent, rather than describing how they will be made competent.
4. An objective describes the key conditions under which the performance occurs on the job. It describes the tools, equipment, or circumstances that will be a part of the performance.
5. An objective describes the standard of acceptable performance; it tells how well someone must perform before you will consider that person competent *on that objective.*

   Each objective, then, will say:
   a. what someone should be able to do,
   b. the conditions under which the doing will occur, and
   c. how to tell when the performance is good enough.

Course objectives are derived from the analysis documents prepared earlier. You will have as many objectives as it takes to describe the important things you want students to be able to do. There will be one objective to describe each of the tasks you want students to be able to perform and one to describe each of the key skills they will need to learn to perform those tasks. (There will be no objectives describing content, facts, or other information you intend to teach. To write objectives about anything but meaningful outcomes would swamp you in an unmanageable quagmire. Items such as instructional content and practice material go into the instruction rather than into the objectives.) Each objective will be written with enough detail so that another professional instructor could turn out students who could do what you want them to do at the proficiency levels you prescribe. The objectives will answer the question, What should students be able to do at the end of the course?

## Warning: Jargon Ahead

Over the past 25 years or so the notion of objectives has picked up jargon like a ship collects barnacles. They have been called behavioral objectives, competencies, outcomes, and performance objectives. Worse, the same objective has been labeled at one and the same time a classroom objective, a course objective, a school objective, a district objective, and a county objective.

But if you describe a measurable outcome you intend to accomplish, that is an objective.

Keep this in mind: they're not called behavioral objectives any more mainly because too many people thought that meant objectives had something to do with behaviorism, *which they do not*. They're not called competencies, because competency means skill rather than intended outcome. The word *objective* doesn't need to be modified by the word *class, course, school,* or *county*, unless *different* outcomes are intended for those *different* entities.

If you describe an intended outcome specifically enough to tell whether it has been accomplished, call it an objective. Period.

## HOW TO DO IT

1. Collect all the analysis documents drafted to this point.
2. While reviewing the task flowcharts, write an objective to describe the performance of each task.
3. Now look at the list of skills that anyone would have to have before practicing the entire task. Write an objective to describe each of those skills. In other words, write a statement to describe the limits of those skills, one that tells how much of each skill is needed by someone intending to perform the task. (Note: If you are an experienced developer, write objectives only for those skills you are certain your students do not already possess.)

   How much detail should you use? Just enough so that someone else reading the objective would understand it the way you do. How to find out? Show your draft to one or two people and ask them to tell you what they think it means. It doesn't matter if they don't understand the technical content of the objective. If they don't say what you want them to say, don't argue. Fix the objective.
4. Test your objectives for completeness. Each one will be good enough when you can answer yes to the following questions:
   a. Does it say what someone will be doing when demonstrating accomplishment of the objective (e.g., writing, solving, disassembling)?
   b. Does it describe the important conditions that will exist while the performing is being done (e.g., "given a wiring diagram"; "given an irate customer"; "using the tools available in hairstyling kit A")?
   c. Does it tell how to recognize when the performance will be considered satisfactory (e.g., "it operates to within + or – two degrees"; "all customer objections

have been addressed"; "correct to within one decimal"; "polished to a 63 finish")?

5. If, as you worked at the above steps, you found yourself writing one or more fuzzies, such as *understand, comprehend, appreciate, demonstrate,* or any other abstraction, complete a goal analysis for each fuzzy. Mark the performances that represent things students cannot yet do, and write an objective describing each of those performances.

6. If you have completed one or more goal analyses during the task analysis, and if you listed one or more performances that students cannot now do, write an objective to describe each performance that will need to be taught.

**Examples:** Here are some examples of objectives. Note that though their form differs (some are written in a single sentence, others in two or more, and so on), they all say something about desired student performance, about the conditions under which the performance will be expected to occur on the job, and about how to tell when the objective has been accomplished (the criterion of acceptable performance).

*Objective #1:* For a subject with which you are familiar, be able to describe the content of a module that would teach a given objective in that subject when given the objective, the target population description, and the skill hierarchy.

Criteria: the description includes (a) the difference between what students already know and must know before they can practice the objective and (b) a description of relevant practice.

*Objective #2:*

|  |  |
|---|---|
| Given: | A prescribed confined space, standard equipment, and two other team members, |
| Action: | carry out a confined-space entry and exit. |
| Criterion: | Entry and exit will meet ATA–7 Safety Practices. |

*Objective #3:*

Given: A Model XXX System, standard tool kit, spares kit, and at least one symptom of a common malfunction,

Performance: return the system to normal operation.

Criteria: The system functions within specs. There is no cosmetic or structural damage to system or to immediate area. No more than one unnecessary spare was used. No complaints were filed by client personnel.

*Objective #4:* Given a Model 7 word processor and typed copy, be able to load the appropriate program and enter the copy at a rate of at least 80 words per minute.

*Objective #5:* Given a patient of any weight, be able to start an IV after no more than two needle punctures.

## Goofing Off with Objectives

If it were not for the obfuscators, the preparation and use of objectives would be relatively simple. We would simply describe what we want students to be able to do and then get on with developing instruction that teaches them to do it. Unfortunately, there is a gaggle of folks who like to make things harder than they are, who like to hang all sorts of danglies on the dashboard of their instruction. "Oh," you hear them saying as they look over your perfectly wonderful objectives, "now that you have written your classroom objectives, you must write course objectives, and then school objectives, and then the county objectives." Huh? They can't be serious! But yes, they actually do try to propagate the fiction that a shovel is not only a shovel, but also a spade, a digger, a scooper, and a dirt-remover. I've seen dozens of instructors faced with this ridiculous task of rewriting the same objective to fit different jurisdictions. And I've seen them get frustrated, and then furious, as well they should.

There are other ways to goof off with objectives. One is to create a "taxonomy" of performance levels, so that instead of saying how well a person must perform, you simply have the objective say "Level B3," or "Criterion level: A2." This looks very precise, until you look at the definitions of these "levels." Then you discover that the criterion is still being kept a secret. Here's an example from one of these "criterion taxonomies." This one is called TPL-2 (Task Proficiency Level). This is how it is defined: "Can do most parts of the task. Needs help only on hardest parts. May not meet local demands for speed or accuracy." How well should a student be able to perform a task with this alleged criterion? You still don't know.

When you write an instructional objective, you are simply trying to communicate something about what you want students to be able to do when they leave you. That's all. If you want them to be able to unscrew a lightbulb while rubbing their tummy, say so and be done with it. Don't let the bedazzlers tangle your objectives with ornaments that are neither useful nor pretty.

Oh sure, you may find yourself having to conform to some bureaucratic demand to write your objectives in peculiar ways. If so, bend a little. Write a clean set that will be useful for your own instruction, and then rewrite them according to the "guidelines" you are expected to follow. Send those on up the line where they will do little harm.

*To Learn More:* See Resources #5 and #6.

# 9 | Skill Hierarchies

**Situation:** *You have drafted objectives that describe what you want students to be able to do at the end of your instruction. You want to develop a tool that will tell you which objectives must be taught before others can be usefully attempted.*

Before plunging into development or improvement of the instruction itself, it will be useful to arrange the objectives into a picture that will help to answer the following questions:

1. What should I teach first?
2. What should be the sequence of modules (lessons) thereafter?
3. Are there skills that *must* be learned before other skills can be attempted?
4. Are there sequencing options that can be left to the student?

These questions are answered in part by constructing a skill hierarchy. Just as the flowchart visualizes the key steps and decisions involved in performance of a task, the hierarchy visualizes the *relationships* between the skills needed in performance of a task.

The task analysis *flowchart* says, "This step is followed by that step, which is followed by that decision, which is followed by that step."

In contrast, the *hierarchy* says, "This skill must be *learned* before that one can be learned" and "This objective is unrelated to that objective, and so these two objectives can be taught in any order."

Though the skill hierarchy isn't the only source of information for answering the above questions, it is an important source. You will find it a useful tool.

For example, suppose that on reviewing your task analyses, you find that students are going to have to learn to fill out certain forms in the performance of the job (whatever it may be). You note also that they are going to have to be able to read English.

Does one of these two skills—"fill out forms" and "read English"—have to be learned before the other can be learned? Or could you teach them in any order? Could students learn to fill out forms if they couldn't read them? Obviously not. So in this case the reading skill *must* be in place before the form-filling skill can be profitably practiced. The hierarchy, which is read from bottom to top, would look like this:

**Figure 9.1**

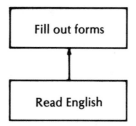

This tells us that all the skills shown leading into the box to which the arrow points should be mastered before that skill can be usefully attempted. We say that the reading skill is *subordinate to,* or *prerequisite to,* the form-filling skill. This does not mean that the reading skill is less important than the other. It means only that it must be in place before the other is attempted. It also tells us something else: it doesn't matter what an instructor alleges to be a preferred style of teaching; the hierarchy shows that one skill *must* be taught before the other one is taught because one *depends* on the other.

Now let's consider another pair of skills. In reviewing your task analysis, you find that your sales students will have to be able to (a) describe product features to customers and (b) operate the product—let's say a car.

Would one of these skills—"describe product features to customers" and "drive car"—*have* to be learned before the other could be attempted? Would I have to learn to describe the features of the car before I could learn to drive it? Could I learn to drive without learning how to describe features to customers? I could, couldn't I? Both skills are important, but it wouldn't matter which was learned first. The hierarchy would look like this:

**Figure 9.2**

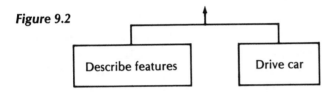

And if you know which skills are independent of one another, you also know which sequencing options you could leave to the student if you so desired. You also have the information that will allow you to maximize the efficiency of a course for which you don't have enough practice equipment to go around. When practice equipment is limited, you can let your hierarchy tell you what students can *productively* work on while waiting their turn for the equipment.

## HOW TO DO IT

1. Refer to the skills you derived from your task analyses. These are the skills you wrote to the right of the task step that requires them.
2. Delete the duplications from that list of skills. For example, it is likely that you will have written "Can read English" or "Use hand tools" several times. If the same reading skill or hand-tool skill is referred to in each instance, delete all but one of them. It makes no sense to teach the same skill once it's learned.

3. Consider any pair of skills. Answer the question, Can these skills be *learned* in any order? If so, you will draw them side by side on your hierarchy. If one must be learned before the other, the subordinate skill (the one that must be learned first) should be drawn below the other, and connected to the other by an arrow.
4. Answer the same question for each pair of skills.
5. Draft a hierarchy—in pencil. (A neat trick is to use those little pads of paper that are gummed on one end. Write each skill on one of the stickies and then move them around until you are satisfied. Then draw your draft in pencil.)
6. Test your hierarchy.
   a. Make sure that every box on your hierarchy describes a skill rather than content. How? If you can put the word *can* in front of each item, it is probably describing a skill. For example, "Disassemble" makes sense when you add *can*—"Can disassemble." "Algebra," however, makes no sense at all when written, "Can algebra." Delete *algebra* and replace it with the skills that are relevant to the performance of the task in question. The subject matter won't get lost; it will go into your lessons. But subject matter has no place on the skill hierarchy.
   b. Starting at the top of the hierarchy, put a finger on each box that has one or more arrows leading into it and ask, "Is it true that students cannot practice this skill [the one you are pointing to] before they learn the skills shown as subordinate to this skill?" If the answer is yes, go on to the next box and repeat the process. If the answer is no, make the necessary correction.

There is more to the matter of deriving hierarchies than can be described here. But the steps above provide the essence of the procedure.

**Example #1:**   This hierarchy shows the skill that must be in place before someone can practice the entire task of baking a cake.

**Figure 9.3**

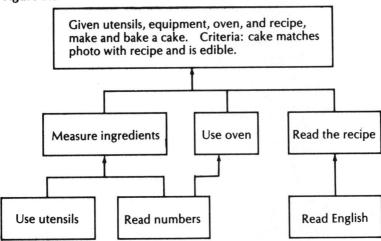

The subskills shown are those that would have to be in place before anyone could be instructed how to bake a cake and before anyone could practice that task. As we have all been victims of those who have *not* had the appropriate subskills in place before practicing the entire task, we should applaud the existence of the hierarchy and virgorously promote its use in the design of instruction.

**Example #2:** Refer to the fold-out hierarchy on the last page of this book. At the end of the chapter on task analysis I showed you the skills needed before anyone could practice three of the steps in the troubleshooting task. Here is what the hierarchy looks like when all the skills required in the performance of this task are put together. Don't let the apparent complexity of this hierarchy blow your socks off. Just look at it a piece at a time, reading from bottom to top.

Notice that the hierarchy does not say anything about any individual person. It shows what *anyone* would have to be able to do before being ready to practice the entire task. Once we know what *anyone* would have to be able to do, then we can match that picture with the existing skills of an individual student and derive a curriculum for that student from the difference.

Note: The dotted lines shown at the right of the hierarchy note skills that may or may not have to be learned, depending on the location of the job assignment.

**To Learn More:**   See Resource #10.

# 10 Course Prerequisites

**Situation:** *You have a clear picture of what students should be able to do when they leave you and a picture (hierarchy) showing which skills are prerequisite to other skills. You can now derive the point at which it would be most appropriate to begin your course.*

Here's another neat way to save development time while making sure that the finished course will do what you want it to: just as you were systematic about deciding where the course should *end* (what students should be able to do when they leave your course), be just as systematic about deciding where it should *begin*. Do it by using the procedure described in this chapter to answer the following questions:

*Who* will be allowed to enter your course?

Will incoming students be expected to fall within certain age limits, have a minimum level of strength, be able to read technical material, perform certain mathematical calculations, be able to speak your language? The answers to these questions represent the prerequisites for your course and will influence where your course begins.

The fewer the restrictions on the entering student, the larger the number of people who will qualify for your course. At the same time, the fewer the restrictions, the more likely it will be that students will differ in important ways. The more restrictions placed on the entering student, the *less* likely you will be to find people who meet your requirements. The trick is to write prerequisites that are realistic.

But let's get one thing straight. "Algebra 101" and "Abnormal Psych" are *not* prerequisites. They may be the names of a couple of courses, and they may be required before someone may enter your course, but they don't qualify as prerequisites to your course. *A prerequisite is a skill that someone must have in order to benefit from your instruction.* If your course is taught in English, then students must be able to handle that language before they can benefit from your instruction. If your course assumes that students already know how to solve algebraic equations in one unknown, then they will be less likely to benefit from your instruction than if they enter it without that skill.

The *name* of a course tells nothing about the skills that students will have when completing the course. A course name describes only an administrative requirement that must be fulfilled; it says nothing about what students should be able to do before entering your course.

## WHERE THEY COME FROM

Prerequisites are derived during course development. Whenever you decide to *assume* that entering students will be able to do this or that, you are establishing a prerequisite. Why? Because prerequisites are formalized assumptions. For example, when you say to yourself, "I'm not going to teach the math they should have learned last semester," it means you are going to *assume* that those math skills are already in place. Since students who do *not* have those skills will be less likely to profit from your instruction, a rule should be established that says "No one may enter this course without the following skills: . . . [such as solve an equation in one unknown; lift at least 50 pounds; climb a pole with climbing irons; name the bones of the body]."

You can see why it is important not to be arbitrary about the prerequisite skills you demand. On the one hand, if you make too few demands and allow everyone in, you will have to begin your instruction at square one. That may be impractical. On the other hand, if you require that too many prerequisite skills be brought to your course, you may not find anyone at all who qualifies. The goal is to be realistic.

Prerequisite skills should be demanded only when necessary. If you have no control over your incoming students and are expected to accept everyone who enters, it is silly to make demands about prior knowledge and skill. The realistic approach is to accept the students who appear on your doorstep and then begin your instruction where they are when they arrive. Sure, you'd rather teach the advanced stuff. But if the students don't have the basics, and if there is no one else to provide them, and if they need them before they can learn the advanced material, you have three choices:

1. Turn up your nose and say, "*I'm* not going to teach them what they should have learned elsewhere," and plow into the advanced material, wasting both your time and theirs.
2. Teach them the basics.
3. Find another way for them to learn the basics while you teach the advanced material.

So set up screening criteria (prerequisites), only when

a. there are one or more things students should be able to do before entering your course, and
b. you have decided it's reasonable not to teach those things in your course.

## HOW TO DO IT

1. Review the task analyses and the list of skills that anyone would have to have before practicing an entire task.
2. Review your target population description.
3. For each skill answer the question, Is it reasonable to expect that entering students will already have this skill?
4. If so, add that skill to your list of prerequisites, and design your course on the assumption that the skill will already be in place.
5. If it is not reasonable to assume that entering students will have this skill, decide how it will be taught: in your course? by some remedial means?

6. Then, as you develop or modify your course, keep an *Assumption List* handy. Whenever you decide to assume that students will know something or be able to do something when they enter your course, add it to the list.
7. If it is reasonable to assume that most students will *in fact* enter your course with the skills described by the assumptions, add them to your list of prerequisites.
8. Write the prerequisites in the form of objectives.
9. Review your prerequisite objectives and make sure that each describes a skill rather than a course name (you are well aware of the wide variations in the way that any course can be taught by two or more instructors).

## A SIMPLER WAY

1. Review your skill hierarchy. (Remember that the hierarchy shows the skills that *anyone* would have to have before practicing the skill shown at the top.)
2. Starting at the bottom, ask yourself whether it is reasonable to assume that your entering students will be able to perform the skill you are pointing to. For example, ask yourself whether it is reasonable to assume that they already can "Read English" or "Use hand tools" or "Add/subtract." (Refer to your target population description for guidance.)
3. If so, draw a circle around that skill.
4. If most or all of your incoming students can be assumed to have a given skill, consider that skill a prerequisite. That is, say to yourself, "I will assume that students can do this when they arrive and therefore I do not need to teach it in my course." Then decide what you will do about those few who do not have that skill—such as provide remedial material.
5. If you have been *told* what skills you must teach, but some of those skills don't *need* to be taught, tell yourself that you will only provide instruction in them for those who may need it.
6. Draw a line across the bottom of the hierarchy that expresses the rule: Skills above the line will be taught in

my course (or somebody else's course); skills below the line will be assumed to be brought by entering students and will therefore be considered prerequisites.

**Example #1:** After reviewing your T. Pop. description, you find that it is reasonable to assume that most or all incoming students will be able to use a word processor to write letters. So you base your instruction on that assumption. You decide not to teach students how to load (boot) or use a word processor. Instead, you will teach only the more advanced applications, and you will turn your assumption into a prerequisite objective, as follows:

Given a Spelgud word processor and one or more draft letters, type and save the letters on the word processor.

**Example #2:** Refer to the fold-out hierarchy on the last page of this book. The target population for a course in troubleshooting consists of people who have had experience in working with a variety of equipment. Though their experience varies, it is reasonable to assume that all of them can perform the skills shown below the line. Those skills, therefore, will not be taught. Instead, they will be considered prerequisites and entering students will be so informed.

*To Learn More:* See Resource #10.

# PART

# II

# Developing the Instruction

# 11 || Criterion Tests

Situation: *You have drafted objectives, a hierarchy, and a target population description. Now you want to develop the tools by which you can find out whether those objectives have been achieved—by which you can find out whether the instruction worked.*

If it's worth teaching it's worth finding out whether the instruction was successful. If it wasn't entirely successful, it's worth finding out how to improve it.

That sounds reasonable, doesn't it? After all, we weigh ourselves to find out whether we have achieved a weight target, we test products to find out whether they are ready to ship to customers, and we measure blood pressure and pulse to assess the state of our health. In the same way, we measure the performance of our students to find out how well our instruction is working so that we can decide what actions to take next.

The most direct measure of instructional success is to determine how many objectives were accomplished by each student. This is done by preparing what is often called a criterion test for each of your objectives. The name is derived from the purpose of the test: to find out whether the criteria stated in an objective have been achieved. In practice, criterion tests are given labels that are most acceptable to the people using them, such as skill checks or performance checks.

The purpose of the criterion test is to determine whether an objective has been achieved, so that both student and instructor can determine what action to take next. If the criteria have been met, the student is encouraged to move ahead to the next instructional unit. If the performance is weak, the instructor diagnoses the problem and suggests a remedy. This use of a test is very different from the practice of "give 'em a grade and be done with 'em." It is a helping purpose rather than a labeling purpose. (Note: Because the purpose is to provide feedback rather than a basis for labeling, you should call it by a name that will be acceptable to your students. "Test" is no good because of all the baggage it carries from our school days. Instead, consider "performance check" or "skill check" or "criterion check.")

The time to draft criterion tests is soon after you have drafted the objectives, but before you draft the instruction. Doing the one soon after the other will help you to clarify your objectives. Whenever you find yourself having difficulty drafting items that are correct for an objective, it will almost always be because the objective isn't yet clear enough to provide the necessary guidance. Clarify the objective, and the test item(s) will fall into place.

Writing the items soon after the objectives will also help you to focus your test items on outcomes rather than on process. It will help you to focus on writing items that will find out whether the outcomes have been achieved rather than on whether students can recognize or recite material that was covered during the instruction.

## CHARACTERISTICS
## OF CRITERION TEST ITEMS

Test items that accomplish the purpose of finding out whether an objective has been accomplished have these two main characteristics: the test items match the objectives in both performance and conditions.

1. Each item matches the objective in *performance*. That is, the performance called for on the test item is the *same* as that called for by the objective (the test asks students to do what the objective says they should be able to do), and

2. each test item matches the objective in *conditions.* That is, it asks the student to perform under the same conditions spelled out in the objective.

And the results of the test are evaluated by comparing the actual performance of the student against the criteria stated in the objective. This means that the student performance must achieve the same criteria as stated in the objective for it to be considered acceptable.

Why insist that a test item match the objective in performance? Let me answer that with another question. Why test? What are you trying to accomplish with your tests? Your answer should be that you want to predict whether students will be able to do what you have taught them when they leave you, not to slap a label on them. The best way to do that is to observe a sample of the *actual performance* you are trying to develop. Anything less than that won't tell you what you want to know. Think about it this way: Suppose your surgeon were hovering over you with gloved hands and the following conversation took place.

Surg:  Just relax. I'll have that appendix out in no time.
You:  Have you done this operation before?
Surg:  No, but I passed all the tests.
You:  Oh? What kind of tests?
Surg:  Mostly multiple-choice. But there were some essay items, too.
You:  Goodbye!

In practice it isn't always possible for your test items to duplicate the conditions called for by the objective. In such cases one approximates those conditions as closely as possible. But it is *always* possible for a test item to demand the same performance as that described in the objective. For example, if an objective asks students to be able to repair equipment under water or to splice cables on top of a pole, it may not be possible to provide the water or the pole. In those instances you would provide the closest approximation to those conditions that you can. But you would *always* ask them to *repair,* and you would *always* ask them to *splice*. The rule is this: If you must, approximate the conditions, but *never approximate the performance.*

## HOW TO DO IT

Prepare a criterion test for *each* objective whose accomplishment you want to measure. Many of those tests will consist of only one item, and the rest will need only three or four. How do you know how many items to include? The rule is this: The test will contain as many items as are needed to sample the range of conditions called for in the objective. Here are the steps for preparing a criterion test.

1. Read the objective and determine what it wants someone to be able to do (i.e., identify the performance).
2. Draft a test item that asks students to exhibit that performance.
3. Read the objective again and note the conditions under which the performing should occur (i.e., tools and equipment provided, people present, key environmental conditions).
4. Write those conditions into your item.
5. For conditions you cannot provide, describe approximations that are as close to the objective as you can manage.
6. If you feel you must have more than one item to test an objective, it should be because (a) the range of possible conditions is so great that one performance won't tell you that the student can perform under the entire range of conditions, or (b) the performance could be correct by chance. But be sure that each item calls for the performance stated in the objective, under the conditions called for.

For example, suppose I am teaching selling and I want students to be able to follow the steps for closing a sale. And suppose I want that performance to occur in the presence of seven different kinds of customers (e.g., calm, angry, hostile, stupid, and so on). I would write an item to test performance involved in closing a sale that would be something like this:

a. Go to video room A, where you will find a "customer."
b. Read the information sheet he or she hands you.
c. When you are ready, turn on the video recorder.
d. Using the product provided, try to close a sale.

Then I would talk to myself like this: "How many times would I want to see that performance before I would agree that students had accomplished the objective? Well, if they could do it once, I'd know they could do it, but if they did it only in the presence of a calm customer, I wouldn't know whether they could do it with a hostile one. I think if I had three samples of performance, I'd be satisfied they could handle the skill under the conditions specified." And then I would write three test items, *each of which called for the same performance* under a different part of the condition range specified in the objective. In the example above, the items would all read the same, but the person playing the customer would be different. One would be hostile, one would be angry, and one would pretend to be a little dull. Most of the time writing test items is simpler than the above paragraph implies.

**Example #1:**   Suppose the objective reads:
Given a Model 12 typewriter, and a standard tool kit, be able to disassemble the typewriter to the frame within ten minutes.
Let's follow the steps listed above.

1. What's the performance called for by the objective?
   *Disassembling.*
2. Draft a test item.
   *Disassemble this typewriter in ten minutes.*
3. What are the conditions stated?
   *Given a Model 12 typewriter and standard tool kit.*
4. Add the conditions to the test item.
   *On table 3 you will find a Model 12 typewriter and a standard tool kit. Use the tool kit to disassemble the typewriter down to the frame. You will have ten minutes.*

5. Can all the conditions be provided as called for by the objective?

   *Yes. No changes needed in the item.*

6. Are additional items necessary?

   *No. There is no problem with conditions and little likelihood the performance could be correct by chance.*

**Example #2:**   Let's try another one. The objective says:

Given a malfunctioning Model 239 atomic bomb, one symptom, and a standard tool kit, be able to repair the malfunction within 30 minutes.

1. What's the performance called for by the objective?

   *Repairing.*

2. Draft a test item.

   *Repair that atomic bomb.*

3. What conditions are stated?

   *A malfunctioning bomb, one symptom, and a standard tool kit.*

4. Add the conditions to the test item.

   *You will find a Model 239 atomic bomb in room 10. Use the standard tool kit provided to repair the malfunction. The problem is that the detonator is showing an intermittent short. You will have 30 minutes.*

5. Can all the conditions be provided as stated in the objective?

   *Not on your life, they can't.*

I can hear you shouting, "I am *not* going to give students *any* kind of bomb to be tested on no matter *what* the objective says!" Good for you. But while I can appreciate your feeling, you'd be only partly right. True, it would be impractical to provide the real thing here, even though they will be working on the real thing on the job. But that should never mean that you will ask for anything less than the performance called for by the objective, in this case, repairing. No matter what else you choose to do, you should ask the students to demonstrate repairing behavior, rather than talk-about-repairing or write-about-repairing. That's the only way you can find out whether the objective has been achieved.

It's the conditions you will modify, not the peformance. So find the closest approximation to the real thing you can, and then ask for the actual performance on that. How about a wooden bomb of some sort? How about a real one that has had the oomph taken out of it? What's your best offer?

> NOTE: If you write your test items according to the above procedure, and if you find yourself saying, "But the test items look pretty much like the objective," you need to have a little chat with yourself. Remember that the object of instruction is to bestow competence just as elegantly as you can manage to do it. The object is not to use trick questions just to make it harder, or to spread people on a curve, or to find out whether students "really" understand. The object is to find out whether they have achieved the objectives you derived for them to achieve. If your test items look similar to your objectives, rejoice. They're supposed to look similar.

## THE MULTIPLE-CHOICE TRAP

There is often a temptation to want to use multiple-choice and true-false items for testing competence. After all, didn't we spend a lifetime in school answering this type of item? Yes, we did. And aren't multiple-choice and true-false items easily scorable by computer? Yes, they are. And isn't that a useful type of item for spreading students out on a curve? Yes, indeed.

But all of that is irrelevant and very time-consuming. The most reliable way to find out whether learners can change a tire is to ask them to do it. If you used multiple-choice or true-false items you might find out what they *know* about tire-changing, but you won't find out whether they can *do* it. And if you used those types of items, who would write them? You? Who would do the item tryouts? You? Writing multiple-choice items is a specialty; it isn't easy to dash off a few items that are unambiguous and that test exactly what you want to test, and without training in this skill you will be very likely to write items that don't follow good item-writing practice. And who would do the scoring? You? If not, who will see to it that the test papers get to the scoring machine, and back again—in a timely manner? You see the trap. Just because someone refers to multiple-choice items as objective—which they are not—that doesn't make them useful, appropriate, or convenient. Worst of all, they practically never tell you whether your objectives have been actually achieved. Remember the surgeon who passed all the written tests on appendectomies?

# EXAMPLES

Here are some examples of objectives and several possible test items for testing achievement of each. The test item that would be appropriate for testing achievement of the objective has been checked. The items not checked may tell you whether students could perform some part of the objective, but only the checked items will tell you whether they can perform as the objective demands.

*Objective #1:*   Be able to type a business letter in accordance with the standards described in Company Manual 10A (pg. 23).

*Test Items:*

1. Describe the five elements of a business letter.
2. On the attached letters, circle the typos and items not corresponding to company policy.
3. Tell how you would instruct a secretary in the preparation of business letters in accordance with company standards.
✓ 4. From the attached copy, type a business letter in the form described in Company Manual 10A (pg. 23).

**Objective #2:**

    Given:   A Model 5 computer, standard tool and spares kits, a VOM, and at least one symptom of malfunction,

   Action:   clear the malfunction.

 Criteria:   Computer is returned to normal operation and functions within specifications.

          There is no cosmetic or structural damage to the computer or surrounding area.

          All paper work is correctly completed.

**Test Items:**

1. Draw a block diagram of the Model 5 computer.
2. Explain how you would troubleshoot a Model 5 computer.
3. List the five most common troubles that happen to the Model 5 computer, and check those that are operator-induced.
✓ 4. The Model 5 computer in room 156 will not boot. Use the tools and spares that are in the room to clear the trouble. When you are finished, complete the Standard Trouble Call Report that you will find on the table.

**Objective #3:** Having written a goal you feel is worthy of achievement be able to derive (write) the performances that, if exhibited, will cause you to agree that the goal is achieved (i.e., write an operational definition of a goal you feel it is important to achieve).

**Test Items:**

✓ 1. Describe the steps in completing a goal analysis.
✓ 2. Select a goal for your course and complete a goal analysis.
3. Review the completed goal analyses in the attached envelope. Circle the items that have been incorrectly described as performances.

*Objective #4:*  Be able to correctly assemble an M-16 rifle, while blindfolded, within five minutes.

**Test Items:**

  1. List the parts in an M-16 rifle.
  2. Describe the action of the M-16 rifle. Also state the history of the rifle and the three combat situations for which it is most suitable.
✓ 3. On the table in front of you is a disassembled M-16 rifle. Put on the blindfold and assemble the rifle. You will have five minutes to make the rifle completely operational.

*Objective #5:*  When approached by a prospective customer, be able to respond in a positive manner (i.e., by smiling, offering a suitable greeting, and by asking how you might be of service).

**Test Items:**

✓ 1. Go to the videotaping room. When the instructor turns on the recorder, provide a suitable greeting to each of the "customers" who will enter the room.
  2. Tell how you would respond in a suitable manner to a customer.
  3. Write a description of a typical customer.

## SUMMARY

To find out whether objectives have been accomplished,

  1. make sure your test items ask students to do what the objective asks them to be able to do and
  2. ask them to do it under the conditions stated in the objective, and then,
  3. consider the objective achieved only when the performance matches the criteria written into the test item(s).

Then remind yourself that if you are going to the effort of incorporating techniques intended to make instruction work, it is important to find out whether that worthy goal has been accomplished.

**To Learn More:**  See Resource #4.

# 12 | Relevant Practice

*Situation: You want to make sure that your students' practice time will be devoted entirely to activities that will promote accomplishment of your objectives.*

If there is one thing at which vocational and technical instructors shine, it is in their understanding of the need for practice. They know that one learns to play the piano by practicing on the piano, rather than by talking about the piano or by answering multiple-choice questions about music. They know that the way to learn to interview or to repair or to dance is to practice interviewing, repairing, or dancing. They know that practice makes their instruction work.

Perhaps less well understood is that the *nature* of that practice influences its usefulness.

## PRACTICE MAKES PERFECT, BUT . . .

Practice is a powerful way to develop skill. But practice by itself is not enough! Practice without information (feedback) to the student about the quality of the practice performance can be worse than no practice at all. You know why. Because the students may spend a great deal of effort practicing and learning and getting better at the *wrong thing*. Therefore it is an instructional error to allow students to practice unless a source of feedback accompanies the practice.

Feedback can come either from external or internal sources. Either you can build into the students' heads the ability to recognize correct from incorrect performance, or you can have another person or device do it. If you are going to build the performance criteria into the students' heads, then you must *prevent them from practicing until this is done.* Plainly put, they must not practice until they know how to *evaluate* their own performance.

If you will have an external source provide the feedback, you must be sure that the person or mechanism providing the feedback knows the performance standards. If another person is to provide feedback, that person must know more than just how to recognize correct and incorrect performance. That person must also be able to offer the information in a way that will not destroy the motivation or self-esteem of the student.

## PRACTICE ISN'T PRACTICE UNLESS . . .

Suppose you saw me practicing the tuba, and said, "Hi there. What are you doing?" And suppose I replied, "Why, I'm learning how to dance." What would you think? Suppose I then said, "Y'know, I've been working hard at this, but my dancing doesn't seem to be improving. Got any ideas?" I think your reply would be obvious: "If you want to learn how to dance, you need to practice dancing." And of course you'd be right—and I'd thank you for not using saltier language in your reply.

That is an obvious example of wrong (useless) practice. Other examples are a little harder to decode. Suppose while learning to be a policeman, you were expected to learn when and when not to shoot (a rather important skill). And suppose the instructor had you practice reciting the law that pertains to shooting. Would that practice help you get better at making the shoot–no shoot decision? You see that it isn't as easy to decide in this case. Knowing the law may be useful information, but it won't improve your ability to make the instant decisions that a shooting situation requires. It wouldn't, in other words, provide *relevant* practice of the skill in question.

## HOW TO DO IT

There is a way to make sure that the practice you offer will lead students to improve their skill. Follow this procedure for each objective. Once you've done it for six objectives, it will only take seconds to do the rest.

1. Write down what the student would be doing when practicing the essence of the objective.

    **Example:** If the objective says, "Be able to assemble schlorks . . . ," you would write "assemble schlorks."

    **Example:** If the objective says, "Be able to write a computer program," you would write "write computer program."

2. Write down the conditions and the things that you would have to provide in order to make the practice happen. (The conditions written into the objective will tell you.)

    **Example:** If the objective says, "Given a set of parts and a standard tool kit . . . ," you would list "set of parts" and "tool kit."

    If the objective says, "Given a prospective customer . . . ," you would write "prospective customer."

3. Write down how you will provide information (feedback) about the adequacy of the practice performance (whether it's OK or not OK).

    **Example:** If the performance can be compared against a list of right answers, write "answer key."

    If the performance can be evaluated against a checklist that describes the key characteristics of the performance, write "checklist of criteria or key points."

4. Given the right answers, or checklists, or modeling, or descriptions of desired performance, could students decide for themselves whether their performance is OK or not (adequacy feedback)? If so, fine. If not, you will have to provide an external source of feedback (e.g., another person).

This much will tell you how you will provide feedback about whether the performance is OK or not, and whether you will need another person to observe the practice. Now you need to think about who or what will *diagnose* performance that is not yet OK. That means thinking about who or what will determine (a) what's wrong with the performance (diagnostic feedback), and (b) what to do to fix it (corrective feedback). Answer these questions.

5. If the student knows that the performance isn't yet good enough, do you think the *student* could decide *what* is wrong with it? If so, fine. If not, you will have to provide an external source of diagnostic feedback (e.g., another person).
6. Knowing what is wrong with the performance, will the *student* know what to do to fix it? If so, fine. If not, you will need to provide an external source of information for corrective feedback.
7. The last step is simply to tote up your answers to the above questions and draft a short description of relevant practice for each objective. This description may be as short as one that says, "Provide tools, schematics, faulty thermostat, list of tolerances of adequate operation. Student will practice repairing." Or a longer list of things may have to be provided to make the practice relevant to the objective, along with an instructor or other student to supply feedback by observing the practice while making marks on a checklist.

Whatever the result, the importance of practice—*relevant* practice—cannot be overemphasized. As you well know, *doing is the key to competence*. Since the conditions under which the doing takes place can be critical to student improvement, it pays to complete this step in the development process with care, no matter what or where you are teaching. Here are some examples.

**Example #1:** Because vocational and technical instructors are almost always more interested in the do-about than the talk-about, thinking through the relevant practice issue is usually done very quickly. This example is typical.

# RELEVANT PRACTICE CHECKLIST

**PERFORMANCE**

**1.** What will trainees be doing when practicing the objective?

> *Replacing parts*

**2.** What do the criteria in the objective talk about?

| | | |
|---|---|---|
| • Product of performance ► | Save the Product | ✓ |
| • Shape of performance ► | Record the Performance | ✓ |

**CONDITIONS**

**3.** What cues/conditions must you provide to make the practice possible (i.e., to meet the conditions stated in the objective)?

> *R-bander engine*     *manual*
> *bench*     *parts*
> *tools*

**FEEDBACK**

**ADEQUACY**

**4.** How will you let trainees know their performance is OK or not OK (i.e., meet the standards of the objective)?

(Check as many times as needed.) ──────►

| | |
|---|---|
| • Description of correct responses | ___ |
| • Modeling of desired performance | ___ |
| • Checklist of criteria or key points | ✓ |
| • Description of desired performance | ___ |
| • _____ | ___ |

**5.** Given those standards, can you rely on trainees to decide if their performance is OK or not OK?

(YES)    NO ──────► Have somebody (or something) provide the comparison of performance with standards ☐

**DIAGNOSTIC**

**6.** If the work is NOT OK, can you rely on them to decide what is wrong with the performance?

YES    NO ──────► Could they tell what's wrong if you model the performance and/or describe common problems?

If YES.. Provide modeling and/or description of common errors (problems) ☐

If NO... Have somebody diagnose the performance ◯

**CORRECTIVE**

**7.** If they know what is wrong with their performance, can you rely on them to know what to do to improve?

YES    NO ──────► Would they know how to improve if you modeled the performance and/or described typical remedies or solutions?

If YES.. Provide modeling and/or descriptions of typical remedies or solutions ☐

If NO... Have somebody provide the remedies or solutions ◯

**8.** Describe relevant practice. Account for all the checks made above, and include all items needed to provide the cues/conditions listed in Item 3.

*Objective:* Be able to replace any component in an R-Bander aircraft engine. Conditions: shop environment, tools and manual available. Criterion: No damage to tools or engine; replacements are made according to R-B procedures.

*Thinking it through* (the checklist on the page opposite is a job aid often used in the preparation of relevant practice descriptions):

"Let's see. The performance called for is that of replacing parts (#1 on the checklist).

"The objective criteria talk about the process of the performance (replacements are made according to R-B procedures) as well as the product of the performance (no damage to tools or engine). That means I should videotape the replacement performance so that the performance will be available for review (#2).

"To make practice possible, I'll have to provide an engine on a bench, some tools, some replacement parts, and the manual. Oh yes, I'll also need a video recording setup (#3). That way students can practice evaluating their own performance.

"Now about adequacy feedback. How can I provide the basis for letting students decide whether their performance is OK or not (#4)? Hmm, I can provide a checklist of key items. That way they can review their videotape to see whether their work matches the checklist items.

"Now about diagnostic feedback. If their work is not OK, will they be able to recognize what's wrong with it (#6)? Yes, they will.

"And finally, corrective feedback. If they know what's wrong with their performance, can I count on them to know what to do about it (#7)? Yes, in this instance I can."

And that's it. So my relevant practice description will look like this:

*Relevant Practice Description:*

Provide:    R-Bander engine
             Bench conditions
             Tools
             Manuals

# RELEVANT PRACTICE CHECKLIST

**PERFORMANCE**

**1.** What will trainees be doing when practicing the objective?

*Writing relevant practice descriptions*

**2.** What do the criteria in the objective talk about?

| • Product of performance ► | Save the Product | ✓ |
|---|---|---|
| • Shape of performance ► | Record the Performance | |

**CONDITIONS**

**3.** What cues/conditions must you provide to make the practice possible (i.e., to meet the conditions stated in the objective)?

*Objective*
*Checklist*
*Something to write the description on*

**FEEDBACK**

**ADEQUACY**

**4.** How will you let trainees know their performance is OK or not OK (i.e., meet the standards of the objective)?

(Check as many times as needed.) ——►

| • Description of correct responses | |
|---|---|
| • Modeling of desired performance | ✓ |
| • Checklist of criteria or key points | ✓ |
| • Description of desired performance | |
| • _____ | |

**5.** Given those standards, can you rely on trainees to decide if their performance is OK or not OK?

(YES) ⟶ NO ——————► | Have somebody (or something) provide the comparison of performance with standards | |

**DIAGNOSTIC**

**6.** If the work is NOT OK, can you rely on them to decide what is wrong with the performance?

YES ⟶ (NO) ——————► Could they tell what's wrong if you model the performance and/or describe common problems?

If YES.. | Provide modeling and/or description of common errors (problems) | ✓ |

If NO... | Have somebody diagnose the performance | ◯ |

**CORRECTIVE**

**7.** If they know what is wrong with their performance, can you rely on them to know what to do to improve?

(YES) ⟶ NO ——————► Would they know how to improve if you modeled the performance and/or described typical remedies or solutions?

If YES.. | Provide modeling and/or descriptions of typical remedies or solutions | |

If NO... | Have somebody provide the remedies or solutions | ◯ |

**8.** Describe relevant practice. Account for all the checks made above, and include all items needed to provide the cues/conditions listed in Item 3.

Replacement parts
Checklist of key points
Video recording setup

Procedure: Students will be asked to replace a series of parts. For feedback, they will review the VTR and match their performance to a checklist of key points.

**Example #2:** For an example of a totally different sort, let's use the skill of writing relevant practice descriptions.

*Objective:* Given an objective and a checklist, be able to write a description of relevant practice. Criteria: the description includes (a) the performance required, (b) critical cues and conditions under which the performance is expected to occur, and (c) sources of adequacy, diagnostic, and corrective feedback.

### *Thinking it through:*

"Let's see now. The performance called for is that of *writing* a relevant practice description (#1 on the checklist).

"All the criteria describe the product of the performance (#2), so there would be no need to record the performance for later review; that is, the objective calls for a written description rather than for the behavior that leads to that description.

"To make practice possible, I'll have to provide one or more objectives for students to practice on and some checklists (#3). That's about all.

"How can I provide the basis by which they can decide if their descriptions are OK or not OK? I can provide a model of a description (#4). It would also help them decide whether their description is OK or not OK if I provided a completed checklist.

"Could students compare their descriptions with those two items and decide whether their performance is OK or not (#5)? Yes, they could.

"There's no problem about diagnostic feedback (#6). If their performance is not OK, they can decide what's wrong with it, provided that I provide them with a model and a description of the common errors.

"Would they know how to correct their work, given the model, the checklist and the description of common errors? Yes, I know for certain they could do that. Therefore I don't have to provide an instructor or someone else to do it for them. And that's it. I'm now ready to write a description of what it would take to provide relevant practice."

**Relevant Practice Description:**  To enable students to practice this skill, I need to provide (a) objectives, (b) checklists, and (c) something to write the description on. For feedback, I need to provide a model of the correct descriptions, completed checklists for each objective, and a description of common errors.

> NOTE: Though it takes only minutes to prepare brief relevant practice descriptions for a batch of objectives, it is a key step in the development process. Without it, it's just too easy to provide wrong practice, partial practice, or no practice at all in the important skills you want to teach.

*To Learn More:*   See Resource #11.

# 13 ‖ Content Derivation

**Situation:** *You have derived objectives and the requirements for relevant practice of the objectives. Now you want to decide exactly what content will bridge the gap between what students can already do and what they will need to know or do before they will be ready to practice the objective.*

Now it's time to decide what goes into the lessons themselves. You know what the important outcomes of the instruction should be, and you know more or less what your students will be able to do when they arrive. You know what is available to you in the place where the learning will occur and the restrictions under which you will have to work. And you know what you will need to do to make relevant practice possible.

So it's time to think about the substance of the lesson. Historically, a lesson has been a burst of instruction that consumed a predetermined amount of time. This fixed amount of time has often been referred to as a "period," and consumes 50 minutes. But by now it should be clear that a unit of instruction that includes everything needed for the accomplishment of an objective would be more useful for students. Thus, it may take ten minutes to complete one objective, and two days to complete another. Putting it another way, during one lesson period a student may complete one or two objectives or only part of an objective. So, to avoid confusion, instead of "lessons," we'll call these units of instruction "modules." The term *module* will be used to denote a coherent whole: all the stuff needed for accomplishment of one objective.

So what should be included as content? What should be left out? How can you decide?

If you were to ask some instructors what a student should know about their specialty, the answer would be "Everything." But that's silly, isn't it? Even if it were possible to know everything *eventually*, there's just no way it would be practical to *teach* everything. So something has to be left out. What should the module include?

A module should include content that represents the difference between what students already know and what they need to know to perform an objective.

In other words, a module will contain (a) whatever is needed to take students from where they are to the point where they can begin practicing an objective productively and (b) the practice and feedback.

The procedure for making this happen is relatively simple. The hard part is getting used to the idea that an existing course may contain quite a bit more content and activities than are needed to accomplish the objectives. My colleagues and I recently found that a group of manager trainees would be better performers if a well-tabbed three-ring binder of information replaced the *entire* 18-week course they were required to attend. This is not to suggest that any or all of *your* courses should or could be replaced by a job aid; it is only to remind you that efficient instruction often requires that at least *some* content of an existing course be dropped. Or saved for another course.

You know how it goes. We all have our favorite topics, war stories, anecdotes, and demonstrations. We like the subject we are teaching, and we are all wrapped up in it. That being the case, discovering that some or all of what we do in the classroom can be better done without can be something of a personal affront. But if we are serious about making our instruction as efficient as we can make it, then we need to think of those "extras" as obstacles rather than as necessities.

The secret to deciding what to put in and what to leave out is to think about module content as a remainder, as the difference between what is already known and what needs to be known.

# HOW TO DO IT

1. Review the objective.
2. Review your description of relevant practice for that objective.
3. Review your target population description, and note what students can already do when they enter this module.
4. Now answer the question, Why aren't they ready to practice this objective *now*, at the time they begin work on the module?

Imagine that a student has read the objective of the module and understands the importance of learning what the module has to teach. Why would that student not be ready to practice that objective right then and there? That's the question to answer. To make it easier, break the question into three smaller ones:

a. Do you believe they aren't ready to practice because they don't yet know *how* to do what they need to do? If so, what do they need to know how to do?
b. Do you believe they aren't ready to practice because there are one or more common errors they are likely to make in their present state of readiness? What common errors?
c. Are they not ready to practice because they don't yet know how to tell when their practice performance is OK or not?

The answers to these questions will tell you what to include. And of course, if there is some "standard" content that isn't needed for answering these questions, leave it out. If you happen to leave something out that should be in, you'll find that out when you test the module. (Note: The reverse is not true. If you put something in that should be left out, testing may not expose it. So it's always better to start "lean" and add content and activities where necessary.) So there's little need to worry about putting too little into your instruction.

NOTE: Here's an important tip on how to complete this step in the development process. Think of yourself as constructing a *summary* of lesson content, rather than an outline of content. Sure, your content will be presented in an organized manner when the module is *finished,* but it can be an obstacle to begin outlining before you have any substance to outline. So just list the content of the module as you answer the questions above. And when you find that for some objectives you will need only to provide practice and feedback, reward yourself. Your students will thank you for refraining from boring them with things they already know, and, if they're an enlightened lot, your administrators will thank you for getting the job done with a minimum of wasted motion. ("But I couldn't let my students out early," I hear you gasping. Of course not. After all, we're not *that* enlightened yet. But you *can* provide a menu of optional activities that students would find interesting and productive if they reach competence before the time is up.)

The technique described in this chapter is a powerful one. Use it for your own instruction, but be cautious about applying it to someone else's. Though you will be able to identify all sorts of unnecessary instruction once you've learned this technique, you would be wise to keep that knowledge to yourself. Nobody likes to be told that there is no need for some—or all—of what they are teaching.

Following is an example of this content derivation procedure. I've tried to pick a subject with which you're not likely to be too familiar so that you won't already be expert at knowing the skills involved.

**Example #1:** Ventriloquism involves a blending of the skills of manipulation (operating the puppet), voice, and lip control. Once these three subskills are fairly well in place, students are ready to learn how to act out a script. Here's the objective, along with the hierarchy to show which skills are in place before they enter this module. (By the way, ventriloquists refer to themselves as vents.)

**Figure 13.1**

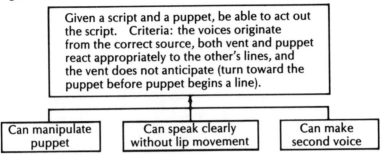

*Relevant Practice Description:* Students will be provided with

- a script,
- a puppet, and
- video equipment.

For feedback, they will review (with an instructor) a video-tape of their performance.

Having completed practice in the subskills, students now enter the module that will teach them to act out scripts. Why aren't they ready to practice when they enter the lesson? They already know how to read, how to produce a voice for the puppet, how to speak using lip control, and how to manipu-late the puppet's controls. So why aren't they ready to practice acting out a script? Well, because they may not know how to recognize correct performance when they see and hear it. They may not be able to recognize a properly acted script. Any other reason they aren't ready to practice? None whatever. This is what a module to teach this objective would contain.

*List of Module Content:*

The objective
*This is what you should be able to do . . . .*
Performance-check description
*Here's how we'll check your competence . . . .*

Description of relevance (rationale)
   *This is why this skill is important* to you . . . .
Demonstration of correct performance
   *Here's how to do it* . . . .
Practice in recognizing correct performance
   *This will help your practice to be self-correcting* . . . .
Practice in performing, with feedback
   *Now it's your turn* . . . .

**Example #2:**   Let's use one of the same examples we used for relevant practice. Here's the objective again and the description of relevant practice for that objective:

*Objective:*   Given an objective and a checklist, be able to write a description of relevant practice. Criteria: the description includes (a) the performance required, (b) critical cues and conditions under which the performance is expected to occur, and (c) sources of adequacy, diagnostic, and corrective feedback.

*Relevant Practice Description:*   Students will be provided with

- practice objectives,
- checklists, and
- paper to write on.

For feedback, they'll be provided with

- a model of correct description
- completed checklists for each practice objective, and
- a description of common errors.

Assume that the target population consists of people who have learned the skills described in the earlier chapters of this book. Now they are entering a module that intends to teach them how to derive such descriptions of relevant practice from any objective. What should that module include?

Without batting an eye, you should answer, "Practice." Right. No matter what else it includes, it will include practice in the objective and feedback (information) about the quality of the practice performances.

What else? Why can't these people practice the minute they walk into the lesson? Let's see . . . they already know how to use the checklist. But they may not understand the importance of the procedure. Second, they may not know when to do it.

Anything else? No-o-o-o . . . wait. Common errors. Without some help they are likely to decide that they will need an instructor to provide feedback, when a less expensive medium would do as well or better. Some practice examples using the checklist will prepare them to describe relevant practice effectively. And that's about all.

So here is what the content of the module would be.

### List of Module Content:

The objective
   *This is what you need to be able to do . . . .*
Criterion test
   *Here's how we'll check your competence . . . .*
Description of relevance (rationale)
   *This is why this skill is important* to you . . . .
Explanation of the procedure and examples of the final product of the performance (i.e., some relevant practice descriptions)
   *Here's how it's done . . . .*
Practice with a series of objectives
   *Now it's your turn . . . .*
Feedback by means of a completed checklist and a model of a relevant practice description that incorporates the items shown on the checklist for each practice objective
   *Here's how to check your own performance . . . .*

The easiest way to learn the skill of content derivation is to practice by applying the procedure to someone else's objectives (quietly and discreetly). That way you get to practice the skill without having your ego bruised at the same time.

**To Learn More:** See Resource #11.

# 14 | Delivery System Selection

Situation: *Having summarized the content for the modules, you are ready to decide how the instruction will be made available to the students.*

Now we arrive at what is probably the easiest part of instructional development, deciding what combination of media we will use to present the instruction and practice to the student. Though there is a priesthood that advocates charts and diagrams and that would have you believe this is a complicated affair, it isn't. For two main reasons. The first one is that you don't have so many choices available to you that you need a chart to help you decide which to use. Bluntly, if you only have two pairs of socks, it isn't hard to decide which to wear. The second reason is that by the time you have listed the things you need in order to provide practice and feedback, you seldom need anything more.

So let's think a little about media selection. First off, instructional technologists talk about delivery system selection rather than about media selection. That may seem as though they're using big words when smaller ones will do, but there is a reason. Media are typically thought of as being *things* such as overhead projectors, blackboards, film, and books. That's fine, except that we use more than that to deliver instruction. We often use people, either to present information, to participate in practice that requires one or more other people, or to assist in offering feedback. In addition, we often use "job things" to assist with instruction in practice, as well as "instructional things" such as workbooks and films. We use

real automobiles for practicing auto mechanics, real heads
when practicing barbering, and real rifles when practicing
marksmanship. Though these are critical requirements for
proper presentation of the instruction, they are not media in
the usual sense of that word. Hence the preference for
"delivery system selection" rather than "media selection."

## FEATURES *vs.* BENEFITS

You already know most of what you need to know to
select a suitable delivery system for the pieces of your course.
You know the features of most of the available media, and
you know what they are used for. That's a big leg up. Before
we move on, though, it would be useful to think a moment
about benefits.

One feature of hydrochloric acid is that it will eat through
metal and cloth. Is that a benefit? Depends on what you're
trying to accomplish. If you're trying to etch metal, it might
be an advantage. If you're trying to quench your thirst, it is
definitely a disadvantage.

One feature of a lathe is that it can make round things. Is
that an advantage? Depends on what you're trying to accomplish. If you're trying to make a table leg, it's an advantage.
If you're trying to make a tin box, it's a useless feature.

One feature of a videodisc is that it can call up a picture
or motion sequence instantly. Is that an advantage? Depends
on what you're trying to accomplish. If you're trying to present
an illustration or demonstration, it can be an advantage. If
you're having it react to a student's learning response, it can
be either a disadvantage or an advantage.

So a feature is a characteristic. A feature becomes a benefit
*only* when it will help accomplish a purpose. (If you keep
that in mind, it will help you cut through the razzle-dazzle
pitches of the bedoozlers and help keep your instructional
costs down.)

Having said that, I can tell you that the rule in delivery
system selection is to *select the most readily available and
economical items that will provide the features called for by
your objectives.*

## HOW TO DO IT

Complete the following steps for each of your objectives. Believe me when I say it won't take long.

1. List the things that will be needed in order to provide relevant practice of the objective. To do this you would look at the things you listed while describing relevant practice requirements. Underline or circle the items that are *things* (e.g., typewriter, disassembled crankshaft, drill press, computer keyboard, tool kit, head of hair).
2. Check that the items selected for practice are those that will allow students to make the most responses (get the most practice) per unit of time.
3. Then if you have other items on the list, decide how you will provide them. For example, if your list says, "List of examples," or "Descriptions of problem situations," write a word or two beside it to say how you will present these items. Will the examples be presented in print? If so, what's the most convenient way to present that print? On paper? On film? On a video screen? If your list says you need a person to assist with the practice, write who that person will be. A student? You? Someone else?
4. If the module will require content in addition to practice, review your content summary and say how you will present the content. Pick a way that has the feature needed for the content involved.
5. Now think about your audience. Are the items you selected appropriate for them? If not, select another medium with similar features. For example, if you have decided to present information in print but your audience can't read too well, pick another medium that demands less reading.
6. Are the items you've listed available to you? If not, select something that is.
7. Are the items you selected easy for students to use, easy for them to get, and easy for them to operate? If not, try to find something more practical.
8. Finally, can you think of items that will give you the feature you need but that are less expensive to buy and to maintain? If so, change your original selection. For example,

although you initially decided to present information by filmstrip, second thought may convince you that a series of explained photos in a booklet would be cheaper to produce and easier to maintain (no batteries or torn film to replace).

And that's it. Sure, there are times when a decision can be a little trickier to make. But most of the time it will be a simple matter of selecting the things you will need to (1) provide relevant practice and feedback, and to (2) present information, demonstrations, and examples. Try not to make it harder than it is.

## Example #1:

*T. Pop.:*  High school students

*Objective:*  Copying typed or printed copy, be able to type at least 40 words per minute. Criterion: two typos or less.

*Relevant Practice Description:*  Provide copy from which to type, a typewriter, paper, place to sit. Feedback: word and error count by instructor or assistant.

*Delivery System:*  Typewriter, copy, typing paper, place to sit. Instruction to be provided by print (a manual).

## Example #2:

*T. Pop.:*  Machinist apprentices

*Objective:*  On a metal lathe, be able to turn brass round stock to blueprint specifications.

*Relevant Practice Description:*  Provide lathe, brass round stock, blueprints. Feedback by instructor or assistant.

*Delivery System:*  Metal lathe, brass round stock, blueprints, instructor or assistant. Micrometer for measuring finished practice work. Instructor to present content (to minimize reading load), supervise practice, and provide feedback.

## Example #3:

*T. Pop.:* Instructional technology students

*Objective:* Given any objective, be able to prepare a criterion test item to match that objective. Criteria: The item calls for (a) the performance, under (b) the conditions described by the objective.

*Relevant Practice Description:* Students will be given objectives and asked to write test items. Feedback: model of correct or acceptable items; checklist of key features.

*Delivery System:* Sample objectives, checklist, and instruction presented in print.

## Example #4:

*T. Pop.:* Sales trainees

*Objective:* Given product information and the product, be able to describe all key features and benefits to a customer. Criteria: All information presented is factually correct, and customer is not insulted or humiliated.

*Relevant Practice Description:* Another student will role-play a customer, and trainee will use product information and the product itself to practice describing features and benefits. Session will be videotaped. Feedback: Student and instructor will view tape while applying a checklist of criteria.

*Delivery System:* A student to role-play customer; videotaping and playback equipment; product information in print; the product itself; instructor to provide information and feedback.

*To Learn More:* See Resource #11.

# 15 | Module Development

**Situation:** *You are ready to draft the instruction.*

A powerful way to organize instruction is to build it around a meaningful outcome, or objective. When students can understand and experience the need for the instruction, they are likely to be more highly motivated, learn better, and retain longer.

Since some objectives take only a few minutes to master and others may take more than a day or two, it is clear that objective-based modules may not fit neatly into a 50-minute period. This is not a problem for those teaching in industry, as students there are enrolled in only one course at a time and can devote their full instructional day to accomplishment of the objectives at hand. They can work as long as necessary on one objective-based unit of instruction and then move to the next when they have demonstrated mastery of the first. If the day ends before they have completed an entire module, they can pick up the next day where they left off.

Less fortunate are the instructors who are constrained by the 50-minute hour and by their students being at the same time enrolled in other courses operating under different rules. Here, students can work only until the end of the short period before being interrupted and then must reorient their attention to a totally different subject. Even so, it is still possible to prepare objective-based modules of instruction for this instructional environment, and some instructors have made it work quite successfully.

# THE FLOOR PLAN

Whether stated or not, every lesson or module has a floor plan. Something happens first, then something else happens, followed by something else. (How's that for specific?) The kind of floor plan you should be shooting for is one that does the following things, in approximately this order:

**Figure 15.1**

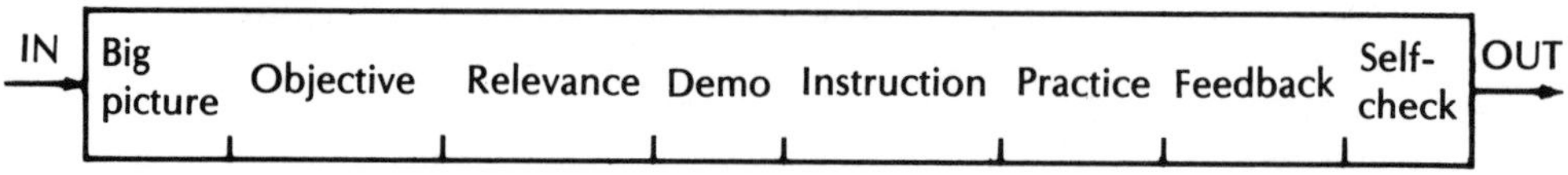

> *Big picture:* Reminds or shows students where they are in the larger scheme of the course. (Always included.)
>
> *Objective:* Shows them the objective they are to accomplish, in terms they can understand. (Always included.)
>
> *Relevance:* Explains and/or demonstrates why the accomplishment of this objective is important to *them*. (Always included.)
>
> *Demo:* Shows what students will look like when performing the objective. (As needed.)
>
> *Instruction:* Teaches students what they need to know before they can practice the objective. (As needed.)
>
> *Practice:* Provides practice in the objective. (Always included.)
>
> *Feedback:* Provides timely information about performance and progress. (Always included.)
>
> *Self-check:* Provides a way to check whether students are ready to demonstrate their ability to perform as the objective requires. (As needed.)

Notice that the floor plan shown above is not media specific; that is, it can be followed no matter who or what presents the instruction. No matter how the instruction is delivered, students should know at all times why they are doing what they're doing and how to tell when they're doing it satisfactorily, and they should be afforded opportunity to practice until they *can* perform as desired.

Different lessons will have somewhat different floor plans, simply because the objectives are different and need different activities to accomplish them. Where one module will have nothing but practice and feedback, another will have considerable guided presentation with information, examples, and demonstrations. Where one can be self-paced, another will need to be group-paced.

## LOCATING EXISTING MATERIAL

It is a waste of time to "reinvent the wheel," so save time by locating existing material that can be used as part or all of the instruction. If it already exists, save your time and use it.

But use only those portions of it that are relevant to accomplishing the objectives. If you make students sit through an entire 30-minute film, for example, when only 3 minutes of it are relevant to the objective, you're not only wasting their time, but you're squandering their motivation to learn. The same is true if you make them read an entire chapter in a text when only one page will help accomplish an objective. The object is to locate potentially useful material and identify those pieces of it that will be directly useful in helping someone toward an objective.

When potentially useful materials include a textbook, you will seldom need to include the entire text. Textbooks are written in a sequence that makes sense to the author, or in a sequence that is a logical presentation of the subject matter. They are seldom written in a sequence that is logical from the students' point of view. Further, they always contain a good deal more content than is needed to accomplish the objectives you have on hand. Therefore, when a textbook includes material useful for accomplishing one or more objectives, that text will usually be used in a sequence other than the one in which it was written.

This is no problem, of course, except when an accrediting agency wants to know why you are using the text "out of sequence" or not using a text at all. If your objectives have been derived from a good analysis, however, you will be able to show the rationale that caused you to select the content that you did. "Or," said one of the kindly souls who helped test the manuscript for this book, "you can always send them one course outline and teach another."

## MODULE SCRIPTS

The way you put pencil to paper when developing a module will depend mainly on how the instruction will be delivered to the students. For example, if the instruction will be delivered by audiotape, you would write the module in the form of a script. If it will be delivered in print, you would write the instruction in a form intended to be read by students.

During the development of the module it often becomes necessary to make concessions to the rules of the institution—to force a few square pegs into round holes, so to speak. If your institution seems to have fixed rules about what students must do during class hours, or if instruction appears to be restricted largely to lectures from the platform, it will be necessary to make more radical modifications than if more flexibility is permitted. But even in the most modern settings there will be constraints of one sort or another, and this is the place to compromise between the ideal and the possible.

Since it is likely that you will be the medium through which much of your instruction will be presented, you are most likely to prepare the module in the form commonly known as the lesson plan.

## MODULE CONSTRUCTION

Here is a sequence of steps to use as a basis for module development.

1. List the materials that will be needed for the module, either by you or the student.

2. Locate existing materials that may be useful, and compare them with the objective of the module. Mark those pieces

or passages that will be directly useful. Put the name or number of the objective on the appropriate passage (you should be able to associate each instructional action with the objective it is intended to accomplish).

3. Begin either by writing the objective itself as it should be presented to the students or by describing and illustrating the result expected. Use language the students will understand at this point in their development.

4. Write a description or demonstration of why it is important *to the student* to develop the competence described by the objective. Remind students of where this objective fits into the larger scheme of things. (Note: Sometimes the importance of the objective is so obvious that little or nothing need be done here. You can't make a dead horse deader by beating it.)

5. If you will be presenting the instruction from the platform, outline the content you will present in one column, and say what students will be doing in another column. List the examples you will use and any practice items needed to teach students how to recognize competent performance of the objective. Make sure that students are active (doing something other than listening or taking notes) during at least two-thirds of the instructional period.

   If the instruction will take the form of a written module put into the hands of the students, tell them what to do. Include directions such as

   - View videotape V-34.
   - Check your answers on the next page.
   - Have an instructor review your findings.
   - Read pages _____ before practicing.
   - Get the performance check and do what it says.
   - Ask an instructor to set up a machine so that you can demonstrate your mastery of the objective.
   - Do the following practice exercise.

- Ask another student to fill out Checksheet W as you conduct the practice interview.
- Ask another student to role-play a customer as you practice the selling skill.
- Read pages 3–4 in the green flight manual.
- Complete pages 5–8 in the workbook.
- Ask an instructor to demonstrate _____ .
- Give your practice videotape to an instructor for review.
- Sign up for the group practice session.
- Sign up for the brazing demonstration.

In other words, make sure that the module directs the student to the instructional sources and to the practice. When few instructional resources exist, they will either have to be created and included in the module or presented by you. In the latter case the module would indicate to students when they should be ready for your instruction on the topic being studied.

6. Write the practice section of the module. Say where students should get the equipment or other practice items they will need, make sure you tell them what to do with those things, and describe how feedback will be provided.

7. Finally, write what students should do to demonstrate their achievement of the objective. If this will entail a paper-and-pencil test, tell them where to get it and how it will be administered. If it entails their demonstration of skill on a machine or with a process, tell them where to go and what to get. In other words, state what they will have to do to be eligible to begin another module.

## THE LESSON PLAN

A lesson plan is an instructional prescription, a blueprint describing the activities the instructor and student may engage in to reach the objectives of the course. Its main purpose is to prescribe the key events that should occur during the module. If the instructor finds it necessary to deliver most or all of the instruction from the platform, the lesson plan is the guide to the instructor's actions. When a module is put into the hands of the student, it performs a similar function: it tells the student what to do, where to locate the instructional resources, how to practice and how to demonstrate competence when ready.

The precise form of the lesson plan is less important than that it performs its important functions. As you have already listed or summarized the content of each lesson, the task of preparing a module, either in lesson plan or student format, will be relatively simple. Whatever the format used, however, make sure it emphasizes what *students* will be doing rather than what you will be doing. That way you won't be likely to fall into the trap of developing a course principally on the basis of what you like to do rather than on the basis of what students need to do to accomplish the objectives.

## IF YOU'RE STUCK

Sometimes our pencils go limp or our brains turn to mush. In other words, sometimes we get stuck. Fortunately, there is a simple solution. Write the practice section of the module first. By the time you've drafted your objective and relevant practice description, you will *always* know what the practice will look like. So start there. Say what equipment and supplies students will have to get, say where to get them and what to do with them, and describe how feedback will be made available. Once you've done that, you will have a much clearer picture of what the remainder of the module should be like.

To be perfectly honest, this is a procedure that you might consider using all the time. Here's why. Just as the writing of a criterion test item is a good way to find out where the objectives need sharpening, writing the practice section is a good way to sharpen your understanding of what else, if anything, will need to be added to the module in the way of content. Just as the result (the objective) tells you what kind of practice you need, the practice will suggest the additional content you will need.

**Example #1:** This example is a module written in the form of a lesson plan for use by someone instructing from the platform.

*Module:* Hairstyling

*Objective:* Using hair-shaping implements and supplies, be able to cut the client's hair to the requested hairstyle.

| Instructor Activity | Student Activity |
|---|---|
| 1. Explain purpose of the skill and when it is used. Describe objective and hairstyles to be learned. | |
| 2. Demonstrate use of each implement. | |
| 3. Hold up implements and ask students to name each. | Respond with names of implements. |
| 4. Demonstrate and explain first hairstyle. | Ask questions during demo. |
| 5. Explain and illustrate common errors and how they are avoided. | Ask questions during demo. Students practice on each other. |
| 6. Correct student errors. | |
| 7. Demonstrate and explain second hairstyle. | Ask questions during demo. |
| 8. Explain and illustrate common errors and how they are avoided. | |
| 9. Correct student errors. | Students practice on each other. |
| 10. Describe common errors and how to avoid or correct them on second hairstyle. | Students ask questions. |
| 11. Initiate individual performance test. | Students claiming to be ready are tested first, while others continue practicing. |
| (Continue with additional hairstyles, if any.) | |

Sometimes it may be appropriate to add an "Equipment and Materials" section somewhere on the lesson plan. This will provide a ready checklist of the items that you will need to complete the lesson without embarrassing glitches. Some instructors prefer to add this section near the top of their lesson plans, while others prefer to add a third column to the lesson plan itself. This third column is used as space in which to list items needed for each of the lesson components.

The main thing to keep in mind in lesson planning is to adopt a format that will help you rather than get in your way. And remember: there is no *instructional* reason why all your lesson plans should look alike. Though you may have a bureaucratic mandate to adopt a particular format, you can always fulfill that requirement and then build a lesson plan in a format that will help you *and* meet the needs of the objectives to be taught.

**Example #2:** This is an example of a module to be presented in print to students in a course that is criterion-referenced (i.e., the instruction has been designed to accomplish specified objectives) and partly self-paced. This module was borrowed from the nine-module course entitled "Instructional Module Development," by R. F. Mager. It is intended for the population of students learning how to be instructional developers and shows them how to prepare the instructions that will be needed when their course will be taught by someone *other than themselves.* This example shows the module in lesson-plan format for use by someone instructing from the platform, and Example #3 shows it in the print format to be given to students.

*Module:* Prepare Implementation Instructions

*Objective:* Given a module of instruction that accomplishes its objective, be able to prepare the directions and instructions that will enable the module to work when administered by another instructor.

| Instructor Activity | Student Activity |
|---|---|
| 1. Explain importance of the activity. | |
| 2. Hand out example module. | Read example module. |
| 3. Ask students to list the items and information they feel they would need before they could teach the sample module. | List information needed in preparation for teaching the sample module. |
| 4. Ask students to volunteer the information on their lists, and ask other students to add items or to comment. | Discuss the lists. |
| 5. Hand out Implementation Checklist. Answer questions about the items. | Ask questions. |
| 6. Ask each student to draft the implementation items and instructions needed by another instructor expecting to teach the module. | Write implementation material. |
| 7. Have student give his or her module and implementation instructions to another student. Ask student to list missing items. | Review someone else's module and implementation material and list missing items. |
| 8. Discuss results of the practice. | |
| 9. Administer criterion test. | Prepare implementation material for a second module the student has already drafted. |

**Example #3:** Here is the same module as in Example #2 written in a form to be handed to students who are working through a performance-controlled, self-paced course in which they are learning to develop modules to be used in similarly conducted courses. In these courses students work at their own pace until they can perform an objective, demonstrate this ability, and then move on to another module.

As you read through the module see if you can identify the following components:

- Objective
- Criterion test description
- Description of relevance
- "Prepare to practice" content
- Practice
- Source of feedback for the practice
- Directions to the student
- Job aid to guide performance

---

*Module:* Prepare Implementation Instructions

*Objective:* Given a module of instruction that accomplishes its objective, be able to prepare the directions and instructions that will enable the module to work when administered by another instructor.

*Criteria:* The directions and instructions answer questions about (a) what to collect in the way of materials, supplies, equipment, resources; (b) how to prepare the equipment, materials, and space for use; (c) how to answer common questions and handle common problems; (d) how and when to suggest alternative resources and activities, if any; and (e) how to review criterion test performance.

*Criterion Test:* Prepare the directions and instructions that would be needed to allow your module to be administered by someone else. Locate two participants willing to assist. Give one of them your module and additional materials, and ask the other to serve as student. Observe the session (without interrupting), and make notes of any assistance you need to offer to make the session work.

The most terrific and fantastic machine in the whole world is useless unless someone knows how to operate it. Unless someone knows what to do with it, it will just sit there gathering dust. Worse, without good operating instructions, people are likely to *misuse* those wonderful devices. They may even damage themselves or others in the process.

Modules are like that. It's one thing to make them work while they are under *your* control. It's something else to be able to make them work when they are under someone *else's* control. It's one thing for you to be able to smooth the path of the learner by offering a resource here or by anticipating a problem there. It's something else to be able to get others to do likewise.

You have done the first part . . . the big part; you've created the modules. You've tested them and revised them and you've made them work. Now it's time to add whatever is needed so that someone else can make them work. And if there is one thing you can believe, it's this: Murphy's law lives; if anything can go wrong, it will. People will administer your module at the wrong time, in the wrong way, without providing the necessary materials or supplies or space. But it's even worse than that. Unless you provide instructors with all the information they need to implement the module correctly, they won't administer it incorrectly . . . *they won't use it at all.* It will go right up on the shelf. After all, the instructor "knows" how to teach the material in your module, and since that way is familiar, it will take precedence over your module . . . unless you make the process of module administration clear and complete, unless you put the words into their mouths that they will say to their students, and unless you tell them exactly what they need to do to prepare and to administer the module.

But what else is there, you may be wondering? After all, you have created modules that are self-contained in that they only need an instructor to provide feedback for practice. What else is there?

Think about it this way.

### The Slot in the Wall
Imagine that you will slip your module through a slot in the wall, to be administered by an instructor on the other side. You can peek through a little window to see what is happening, but you can neither talk to the instructor nor use body language to signal what should be done next. All you can do is to slip your package through the wall and watch.

What would happen? The instructor picks up the package

and fingers through the pieces. What will he or she do then? Would this instructor know whether there are some preparations that need to be made before giving the module to a student? How would this instructor know what to read or look at first? Would this person know

- what to collect in the way of equipment, supplies, and materials, or resources?
- what sort of environment to arrange?
- how to prepare equipment for practice?
- how to schedule students for practice on scarce equipment or other resources?
- how to anticipate and handle common problems or questions?
- how to review practice exercises, if any?
- how to review criterion test performance?
- when and how to suggest alternative resources and activities?

If the answer to any of these questions is no, then something is missing and needs to be added. Usually, this will consist of a "Note to Course Manager" in the self-evaluation material or in the *Course Manager Manual*. Sometimes it will mean drafting a list of supplies that need to be collected. When students will have to be scheduled for time on equipment or for use of a room, it may mean drafting a sign-up sheet or instructing instructors on how the scheduling should be done and how it should be used. And unless you prepare and provide the answers to the above questions, you should expect that your module will be laid aside rather than used as you intend.

You see, you are now dealing with a target population different from the one for which your module was created. You are dealing with the audience of instructors, rather than of students. You are now trying to package your module in such a way that the instructor population will know how to implement the instruction you created for your student population. Quite a different matter from "packaging" a module that will teach an objective. It's the difference between creating a highly flexible computer and creating the instructions that will allow someone to use it. It's the difference between creating a gourmet dinner and creating the recipe that will enable others to re-create that same gourmet dinner. It's the difference between creating a fantastic jazz solo and writing the sheet music that will cause others to play it the same way you do.

So to make your module usable by others, it will need to be accompanied by whatever directions or instructions will allow others to follow the same implementation steps that you do. And those instructions and directions will need to be just as specific as you can make them. If you are writing instructions for a role-play, for example, rather than simply suggest that the instructor "Give the participants a little pep talk to get them in the mood," tell them exactly what to say. Put the words right in their mouths. "Say to the participants the following. . . ." Whenever you have to provide directions or instructions for someone *else* to give to students, be as precise as you can.

Here's an example:

**For the Instructor**
1. Get the practice envelope marked R-1, and check to see that it contains the five drawings labeled 1 through 5.
2. Set the controls on the white print machine to accept a medium-density drawing.
3. Hand the envelope to the student, and say to the student: "Here are five typical jobs to be run on your white print machine. Tell me how you would set up the machine to run ten copies of each drawing."
4. Write the student's response in the space provided on the response sheet.
5. If the student's response for the first drawing is correct, say, "good." If it is not correct, tell him or her what the correct response is. (This is a practice session, not a test.)
6. Provide this type of feedback as each item is completed.

Though you may not have to do this sort of thing often, when you do, be precise.

And now, before drafting your own implementation material, it will be useful to look at a few other examples.

**Here Is What to Do**
1. Ask the course manager to lend you a copy of the *Course Manager Manual* booklet for this course.
2. Review the table of contents to note the types of information contained in the manual.
3. Read the section labeled "Module Notes." Note the types of information and comments included there.
4. Review your own *Course Control Documents* booklet. What type of information included there would help an instructor to administer your module?
5. Borrow the module of a colleague who is also working through this course. Pretend that you will be teaching that module as part of your own course. List the types of additional information that you would want to have before administering the module to a group of students in *your* learning environment.
6. If you have followed the steps described above, you should be ready to tackle the instructor directions for your own module. It may be easier to do if you break the task into four sections and deal with them one at a time.
   a. *Materials collection*
       In a large number of instances a module will simply need to be made available to students; not only is the module self-contained but all the items needed to make the module function are enclosed within it. Others require the use of equipment or materials or resources. Someone has to be directed to collect these items before the module can be used.

       Is everything the student will need contained within the module itself, within the package of print or tapes or discs you have drafted?

       Does the student need to use something, fix something, adjust something, fill out something? List those somethings as the items that will need to be collected before the module can be attempted.

b. *Preparation*

If you only have one Limpmobile for each ten students and if each student has to practice replacing the Inlaw Ejector, someone is going to have to schedule the practice time. Can it be accomplished by a simple sign-up sheet hung on a door or wall? Will another method be needed? However it is to be accomplished, an instructor or someone will have to prepare the mechanism by which the practice will be scheduled.

Will students need to fill out forms? Will they need to travel to where the equipment they are learning about is located? If so, where will the forms be placed? How will students get to the equipment location?

Will students be expected to practice troubleshooting equipment? If so, what kind of practice "bugs" (troubles) should the instructor insert? In what order? Clear directions will need to be prepared for the instructor preparing to administer the module.

c. *Implementation*

Sometimes the instructor will have a role to play while the module is being attempted by a student. It may be that the course manager will be expected to review a practice exercise or perhaps to demonstrate a procedure. If so, the course manager should be prepared for these activities; instruction on how to handle these activities should be made available.

Are there typical questions that students will ask, common problems to watch out for? Are there typical errors during practice? If so, draft some comments designed to help the course manager implement the module the way you would like to have it implemented.

d. *Evaluation*

When a criterion test involves responding to a number of questions for which there are right or wrong answers, students are encouraged to compare their responses with those that are contained in the self-evaluation materials. But what about all those instances in which a criterion test asks for original or creative responses or asks students to write something, draft something, make something, say something? The course manager will be expected to review the work and to determine whether the perfomance is OK or not yet OK and provide diagnostic, and perhaps corrective, feedback.

The criterion test for this module, for example, asks you to prepare the directions and instructions that may be needed to implement your module and to take that material along with your module to a course manager for review. Two things have been done to prepare the course manager to handle this review. (1) A Module Note in the *Course Manager Manual* describes the activity and offers hints in handling typical omissions. (2) A checklist of items to look for is included in the self-evaluation material.

Do you have self-evaluation material written for your criterion test? Is it self-explanatory, or would a course manager benefit from some directions or comments from you about how to proceed?

**Your Turn**
If you have followed the instructions on the previous pages, you should be ready for the Criterion Test (be sure to read it carefully before you begin), which will ask you to prepare the items that will be needed before the module can be implemented by someone other than your self.

You will be expected to hand your module and the instructions to a collegue, who will in turn be expected to administer the module successfully to another workshop participant . . . *without help from you.*

## Module Implementation Checklist

1. If materials are used in the module, is there a materials list for the course manager?
2. If materials are used, are there instructions on how they should be set out or prepared for use?
3. If equipment is involved, are there instructions about how to locate and set up the equipment?

4. If troubleshooting practice is involved, are there instructions on exactly what practice troubles to use and in what order? Are there instructions on how to set up the practice session?

5. If equipment or space must be shared, is there information on how to schedule the time?

6. Is there information on how to handle common questions or problems?

7. Are there directions on how to handle practice exercises, if needed?

8. Is there information about how and when to suggest the use of alternate resources and activities?

9. Are there suggestions on how to review criterion test performance?

# MODULE CHECKLIST

Use this checklist to assure that your modules include all the components they need for facilitating the performance you want.

## DOES THE MODULE

1. have a title or label? _____
2. show the student the objective in terms he or she can understand? _____
3. describe what the student will have to do to demonstrate competence? _____
4. describe or illustrate the place or relevance of the objective in the larger scheme of things (if needed)? From the *student's* point of view? _____
5. demonstrate or show what the student will be like when performing the objective (if demonstration is needed)? _____
6. prepare the student to practice (if demonstration is needed)? _____
7. include relevant practice of the objective? _____
8. provide the tools, items, objects needed for relevant practice? _____
9. provide relevant feedback for the practice? _____
10. practice what it teaches—or are there modeling errors? _____
11. show trainees exactly what to do or where to go at each point in the module; are there adequate directions? _____
12. help trainees decide when they are ready to demonstrate their competence? _____
13. use the simplest possible delivery system? _____
14. flow from beginning to end; does it have continuity? _____
15. contain no unnecessary obstacles between the student and the learning? _____
16. have a criterion test and associated self-evaluation (feedback)? _____

If you follow the how-to-do-it steps described in this chapter, you will find the job of drafting your instruction greatly simplified. You won't have to anguish over what content to include and what to exclude, because you will have guidance to point you in a productive direction. Do what you have to do to get students entering the lesson ready to practice, and then provide that practice along with some appropriate feedback. When they can perform according to the criteria stated in the objective, say something positive and then encourage them to move on.

> NOTE: Following this procedure will in no way restrict your ability to make your instruction interesting and motivating. To the contrary, students always seem more interested in instruction they perceive as being relevant to their needs or desires. And don't be concerned that "lean" development will take the heart out of the instruction. No matter how tight you make your instruction, there will always be some slack in it for transitions, extra examples, war stories, and anecdotes. But with properly constructed instruction you will always know that no matter how much or how little you embellish, the instruction will do what it is supposed to do.

**To Learn More:** See Resources #11, #14, #15, #16, and #18.

# 16 Sequencing

**Situation:** *Modules have been drafted, and you want to determine the most efficient sequence in which they might be offered to students.*

Since not everything can be learned at once, instruction must be offered in some sort of sequence. One thing must come before another. How shall we decide on the order in which the skills are to be developed? What would be the most beneficial sequence from the student's point of view?

## DISORDERLY SEQUENCE

Before answering these questions, it would be useful to consider the nature of sequence and order. Think about it this way. Imagine yourself sitting at a table that has a box of children's blocks sitting on it. Your task is to make a single stack of blocks. Obviously, you must place them one at a time. That is, first you must put down one block, and then you must put another one on top of it, and so on. But you don't necessarily have to pile them in any order. As long as one block is on top of another, it doesn't matter which block comes before some other block.

If, on the other hand, you were asked to pile them up alphabetically, then the order in which you piled them *would* matter. You'd have to put down the A before the B, and the B before the C.

What does this have to do with instructional sequencing? Just this. There is always a sequence of lessons; that is, one lesson always follows another, but there doesn't always have to be a prescribed *order,* that is, they don't always have to be studied in the same sequence by each and every student. To understand this point, look back to the example skill hierarchy in Chapter 9. Notice how many of the skills are independent of one another—that is, shown side by side. Though all of these skills must be learned before the terminal objective (the one at the top) can be practiced, the *order* in which they are learned doesn't matter. And when the order doesn't matter, it is better to let the students decide on the sequence in which they will do the learning. Having some control helps their motivation to learn.

## GUIDELINES

Traditionally, the only guidelines for sequencing instructional activities have been "teach your lessons in a logical sequence," and "teach from the simple to the complex." That's about as helpful as telling someone to "be good." Those rules are just too vague and have too many possible meanings. After all, *everyone* believes they teach in a logical sequence. But if you look to see what they are in fact doing, you will find that some use a historical sequence: they teach what happened first and then what happened second, and so on. Others teach "theory" before practice. Others claim to teach from the simple to the complex but use a sequence that is opposite to the one they would use if guided by the students' definition of simple to complex. And so on.

Fortunately, we can now take most of the guesswork out of sequencing. Here's how.

## HOW TO DO IT

The goals are to inflame the students' interest in the subject, keep their motivation high, and make sure they have accomplished the course objectives by the time they leave.

1. Begin the course with the topic of highest interest to the students, regardless of where the full treatment of that topic falls within the course. Imagine you have signed up for a course in locksmithing because you want to learn to pick locks like the detectives on TV. You show up for the

course ready and eager to get started. You flex your fingers and get ready to pick your first lock. But the first week is on the history of locksmithing, the second covers the theory of locks, and the third is on assembly and disassembly. By then there are cobwebs under your armpits, mildew on your brain, and you're wondering why you came.

No matter what the item of highest interest to your students, begin there. Jerk them into the course by giving them a taste of the goodies. Spend at least half an hour on that topic, and let them know that there will be more about it later. Then, try to sprinkle the items of high student interest throughout the course.

One instructor I talked with recently couldn't understand why students were uneasy with his course by the end of the first day. Though it is a well-designed and well-developed course, they still felt frustrated. "What they *want* to do is to share their experiences with one another," he said. (These were auto dealers attending a seminar.) "If that's what they really want," I suggested, "start there. Begin with a session during which they are encouraged to share. Then let them know there will be time for more of that, either in the classroom or in the lounge." Don't keep the good stuff hidden until students have "learned the basics."

2. Move from the big picture into the details. Since *you* know the subject, *you* can think comfortably about any piece of it and understand where it fits into the whole. Students don't have that luxury. They don't know the territory and need a map. That's what you're there for. So start with the biggest picture and then work toward the details. If equipment is involved, give your students an opportunity to get their hands on it and, if possible, teach them how to operate it before you teach them anything about how it works.

3. Give your students as many opportunities as possible to decide for themselves which module to work on at any given time. It will help keep them motivated. Naturally,

the constraints imposed by the skill hierarchy and by your environment will dictate how many such options you can offer. The easiest way to let them know what the options are is by means of a course map. Such a map shows the entire course at a glance and shows which sequencing options are available at any given point in the course. Even if you don't have the freedom to provide sequencing options at the moment, you should know how to read and construct a course map.

## The Course Map

A course map is a simple graphic device through which to communicate some of the course procedures to your students. It shows each of the modules and the dependency relationship between them. For example, an arrow between two units tells students that they should first study the unit from which the arrow leads.

**Figure 16.2**

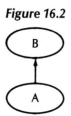

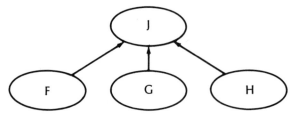

*Master Module A*
*before attempting*
*Module B.*

*Master Modules F, G, and H*
*before attempting Module J.*
*Modules F, G, and H*
*may be mastered in any order.*

A course map also tells students that they should not study any module that has arrows leading into it before they have mastered *all* the units from which the arrows originate. And it tells them that modules shown in parallel may be studied in any order. Here's how to derive a course map from your hierarchy, your experience, and your knowledge of local constraints.

1. Get out your hierarchy and put the name of each module or skill on a quarter of a three-by-five card or scrap of paper (the little stickies—pads of paper with self-adhesive on one end—are ideal).

2. Push these bits and pieces around on a flipchart-size piece of paper until they depict the same relationships shown on your hierarchy. That's where you begin.

3. Now think about the flow of the course. For example, if there are two skills that can be learned in any order, but your experience tells you that one of them should be attempted before the other, just move that module an inch or so toward the bottom of the paper. The two skills will still be shown as independent, but the student will be guided to study the one closest to the bottom of the page before starting on the other.

   If there are two or more independent objectives that should be accomplished before a third is attempted, draw arrows to show this dependency relationship. Students would then know that they can learn the two independent objectives in any order but that they would have to master both of them before attempting the third.

4. When you have all the items in a position that your experience and knowledge of the learning environment says will work, draw the map on the paper *in pencil*.

5. Explain your map to someone—anyone. Talk them through the map from bottom to top. Try to convince this person that you haven't imposed more sequencing restrictions than your subject matter and circumstances require. And then make the changes indicated.

**Example #1:**   Here is a course map showing the sequence of modules to be completed by the students in our self-paced "Instructional Module Development Workshop" from Chapter 15. Notice that though a couple of sequencing options are open to the student, the order of the lessons in this course is mostly prescribed. This is because they are to apply each skill to their own instructional project *in the order* in which these skills are used when developing a course.

**Figure 16.2**

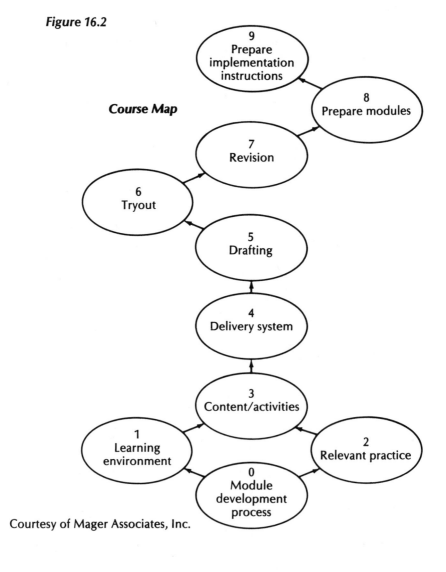

Courtesy of Mager Associates, Inc.

**Example #2:**   Here is a portion of the course map used in the self-paced "Criterion-Referenced Instruction Workshop" (Resource #10). Notice that students have many options in sequencing their instruction. Though it is suggested (but not required) that they begin with modules closest to the bottom of the map, they are encouraged to work on whichever unit is of interest at the time.

Note: The dotted lines with arrows indicate optional modules, and the horizontal dotted line tells students to complete all modules below the line before attempting those above the line. The bold ovals indicate the highest level skill (terminal objective) for that subject.

**Figure 16.3**

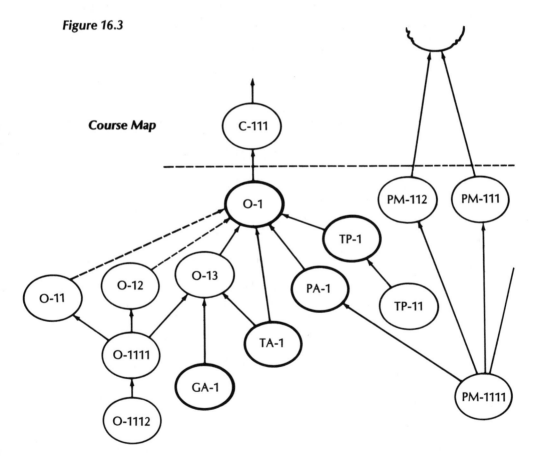

**Example #3:**   Here is the course map from a course called "Developing Performance Aids," created by Peter Pipe. In this instance the meaning of the dotted line is this: the units below it are to be read, studied, and discussed, but because they are informational only, there are no performance checks (criterion tests) associated with them.

The placement of modules DT-1 and ED-1 on the map say to the student, "While it is true that these modules have no prerequisites and may be studied at any time, you will find it more productive to study them sometime after you have completed module PA-1." The placement, in other words, expresses the best wisdom and experience of the author about when those modules might best be attempted. Why then didn't the author draw a line between PA-1 and the other two modules? Simply because he didn't want to falsely suggest that PA-1 *must* be learned before DT-1 and ED-1 can be learned.

**Figure 16.4**

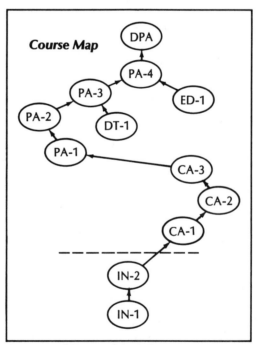

Courtesy of Pipe and Associates

**Example #4:** Many years ago, when I taught introductory psychology at a university, all of us on the faculty *knew* what entering students were interested in. They were interested in sex, ESP, hypnosis, and the behavior of that weird roommate. But where did we begin the course? Why, with the history of psychology. We told them about the good old days when the crazies were chained in dungeons and about how . . . zzzzzzzzzz. And then we would sit around the faculty lounge grousing about how students weren't motivated like when *we* went to school and mumbling about things we could do to wake them up. Dumb.

What should we have done? We should have started right on the first day with one of those topics of high interest. We wouldn't have had to do much with it, but it would have tugged the students further into the course.

You don't arouse anyone's interest with the history of anything. Once you *have* aroused interest by helping them develop some skill and thereby some confidence, *then* students may become interested in the history. After all, learning about the history is one of the ways of "fondling" a subject; it is one form of approach response. But don't ever begin a course with history (unless it's a history course). Tell yourself that until students know something about the subject and have developed at least some feeling of competence, history is interesting only to you.

**To Learn More:** See Resource #2.

# 17 ‖ Tryout

Situation: *Modules are in the process of being drafted or have already been drafted. You want to know how well they work and what to do to improve them.*

Unless you've got a license in mind reading, tryout is the key to instructional success. Oh sure, I know there isn't time for "that sort of thing." I know that in industry lead times are usually short and in vocational and technical institutions instructors aren't given much time for course development. But that doesn't alter tryout being the key to success. I know you would agree with me if I were talking about anything other than instruction—in many instances you wouldn't buy the product if you thought it *didn't* go through tryout.

"Has this airplane been tested?"

"What?"

"Has this plane gone through tryouts to make sure it works?"

"We don't have time for that. We consider the maiden flights the tryouts."

"Oh."

Or,

"Has this medicine been FDA-approved?"

"What?"

"Has this medicine been tested and approved safe to use?"

"No need for that. We find out on the first few patients who die from it."

"Oh."

You see the point. No matter how good we are at instructional development, we still don't know for sure whether, or how well, the instruction will work until we try it out. If there is no time for a tryout before a full class of students shuffles in, then the maiden course will have to be considered the tryout. But don't set the materials in concrete until the results of at least one tryout are in. Make only enough copies of things to take you through the first cycle. Believe me, you will want to fix some things before anyone else sees or experiences it. I'd rather have the errors and opportunities for improvement pointed out before "going public" rather than after, wouldn't you?

## HOW TO DO IT

You already know how to conduct a course, so there's little to tell you before you will be ready to conduct a tryout. The main thing you need to know is that the answers to your tryout questions are readily available for the asking. Whatever you may want to know about how well your course is working or how well it fits your audience, your students will be happy to tell you. And why not? The instruction is being developed for their benefit, so they should be consulted on how well the job has been done.

After all, when your physician whacks you on the back and asks, "Did that hurt?" he or she is asking you for information. When a shoe salesclerk asks you how the fit feels, information is being requested. So be sure to include your students as a key source of information about how well the instruction fits and about how well it works.

There are two kinds of tryout. The first is a check of the individual module or lesson plan. It involves trying it out on one person at a time, until all the major kinks have been removed. The second is a tryout of the entire course. Here's how.

### Self-Paced Module Tryout

Try out each module on at least one person before you test the entire course. Find someone (*one* person at a time: if you use large samples at this point you're wasting your time and theirs) as close to your target population as possible. If a member of your target population is available, fine. But it isn't necessary. As long as you find someone similar to your t. pop. who cannot perform the objective, that person will be a big help. But do a tryout even if the person most available cannot understand the technical language of the module or doesn't fit the t. pop. in other ways. That individual will still locate oversights and errors that you will want to correct before you do a full-course tryout.

1. Locate someone who is willing to work through the module.
2. Write out your instructions to that person. Tell that person that this is a test of the instruction rather than of the person and that you are looking for ways to improve the module. Say that he or she should make a mark on any part of the material that is difficult or that is a turnoff, or that is bothersome for some other reason.
3. Let the person read the instructions, and answer any questions that might arise.
4. Give him or her the materials, show where things are located (if appropriate), and then back away.
5. Sit in the corner and *do not interfere* with the tryout. Do not offer information when you see that the tester is in trouble. Instead, make a note on your pad.
6. If you are asked a question, answer it and *make a note.* Never intervene unless you make a note about the reason for the intervention. These notes will tell you what you will want to do to smooth out the instruction.
7. When the tryout is over, *listen* to the comments of the tester. You can always ignore the suggestions if you choose; you cannot ignore suggestions you don't have.
8. When the tryout is finished, thank the tester profusely, and be sure to add the tester's name to the list of those who helped in shaping the instruction. Be sure to spell the name correctly.

## Instructor-Led Module Tryout

If yours is mainly a lecture-driven course, the tryout pattern is somewhat different.

1. Find a colleague willing to help.
2. Ask the colleague to compare each of your lesson plans to its objective and answer the following questions:

   a. Will students be shown the module objective in terms they will understand?
   b. Will the importance of the module be explained or demonstrated?
   c. Is practice offered in the objective?
   d. Does there appear to be more content than needed?
   e. Will students be doing something other than listening to the instructor for more than 75 percent of the time?

Notice that this procedure does not ask your colleague to dictate or in any way interfere with your style or method of instruction. It merely provides an external pair of eyes that will help you to spot the holes you may have missed while you were putting the modules together.

## Technical Review

It is always helpful to have a colleague or three look through the material to make sure there are no technical errors. If you really need help with the technical accuracy, you might consider the colleague review before the module tryout. If you just want to make sure you haven't made any big boo-boos, then do it afterward. The procedure is the same as that described above for the self-paced course, except that you would not need to watch the review. You would hand, or send, the materials to the colleague along with appropriate instructions and request for assistance. And you would be certain to follow Step 8 above.

**Caution:** Though asked for comments on *technical* accuracy, your colleague may feel compelled to make comments on your instructional approach: "That's not the way I teach"; "It's never been done that way"; "You've left out some of the theory." Your response should be to smile, thank the individual for the assistance, and then feel free to ignore all but those comments that relate to technical correctness.

## Course Tryout

When each of the modules has been tried out at least once and revised on the basis of the information collected, you will be ready for a full-course tryout. Here's how.

1. Collect all the things you will need to conduct the course. Refer to the modules; they should each begin with a list of the items required for the instruction. If you don't have everything you need and that you think is reasonable to expect, or that you were counting on, use the professional approach to procurement: hold your breath, throw a tantrum, throw yourself at the feet of your department head, and plead for the items you need. If you're in the military, the term "midnight requisitioning" may be appropriate here.

2. Duplicate enough materials for the first run-through. No more.

3. If other instructors or assistants will participate in the tryout, walk them through the procedures. If they are going to assist with the instruction itself, give them some practice in handling the portions they will be assigned.

4. Make a copy of the course procedures (described in the next chapter) for each student.

5. Put everything in its place, and then check your preparation.

6. Get a notebook (five by eight inches or larger) and in big letters write on it, "Comments and Suggestions."

7. Place this book in a prominent place in the classroom (your desk is fine for this).

8. When the students arrive, welcome them, tell them which course this is (in case they thought they were waiting for a bus to Fresno), hand out the copies of course procedures, and explain them briefly.

9. Tell them that this is an update on an existing course or a new course, whichever is true. Then tell them that you are sincerely asking their help in improving it. If it's an update, assure them that what they're getting is at least as good as it used to be. Show them the comments book

and encourage them to write their comments in it. If they make suggestions directly to you during the course, thank them and then suggest they write it in the notebook. They will feel more rewarded for daring to make a suggestion.

10. Conduct the course—according to the procedures you have given the students.

11. When it is over, review the comments in the notebook, along with the notes you made yourself.

12. Make the indicated revisions. If there were a lot of revisions, then consider the next cycle a second tryout and repeat the procedure. Go to press only when the indicated revisions are minor or only cosmetic in nature.

One mark of the professional is the insistence on tryouts before "going public." Just as plays are tried out off-Broadway, night club acts polished in the smaller lounges, and products tested until they meet specifications, instruction is put through tryout before being considered ready for regular consumption. The time you spend on tryout is time you will never regret.

**To Learn More:** See Resource #11.

# PART

# III

# Implementing the Course

# 18 | Course Procedures

Situation: *You want to make sure that your course is implemented with procedures as close to the state of the art as your circumstances will allow.*

The technique described in this chapter is one you can implement at any time, regardless of what you may have done before. It will allow you to tune up your course procedures and to capitalize on everything you have done to now, and it will help you minimize the obstacles to learning.

Though they may or may not be written down or recognized for what they are, every course operates by a set of rules or procedures. In one course the rule will be "Tests will be given on the following dates _____ ," while in another the rule will be "Take the test when you feel you have accomplished the objective of the module." The rule in still another course may be "Add your name to the sign-up sheet and you will be notified when the test has been prepared." And so it goes. We have rules about when to arrive, when to leave, how to proceed, where to find things, how to get questions answered, and dozens of other things.

Whatever the procedures by which your course will be conducted, *they should be written down and in the hands of the students.* This will tell them what is expected of them and will eliminate their need to waste time psyching out the instructor. In addition, the very act of writing the course procedures will help you to derive the most efficient implementation strategy possible for the constraints under which you must function. Whatever you do, prepare a set of course procedures for your students and include them as the number-one item in every students' package of materials.

## DERIVING COURSE PROCEDURES

But where do these procedures come from? How are they derived? After all, you wouldn't just sit down and dream up a set of rules at random. Neither would you write a set of rules that reflects the philosophy of "I'll teach *them* the same way that somebody taught *me*." That would be the lazy way out and probably would result in instruction 20 years behind its time.

So how *do* we derive course procedures? We do it by developing rules that put ideal characteristics into practice as closely as local constraints will allow. This means that you compare an ideal or desired course characteristic with your own situation (space, equipment, budget, time, students) and then write one or more rules that will come as close as possible to implementing that ideal characteristic.

These ideal characteristics are derived from research and experience; they represent statements that describe what we would be doing if we developed and implemented our instruction in the very best way we know how. Here are some of the ideal characteristics.

### Ideal Course Characteristics

1. *Instruction exists only where it is a solution or remedy for a problem in human performance.* If they already know how to do it, they don't need instruction. If they don't *need* to learn how to do it, they don't need instruction.
2. *Instructional objectives have been derived from competent performance on the job and adjusted according to the level of competence desired by those who will receive the graduates.* This guarantees a need for the instruction and answers the question, How much _____ should I teach?
3. *Each student studies and practices only those skills not yet mastered to the level required by the objectives.* As a result, you won't waste time and student motivation by

teaching them things they already know, and you'll give them enough practice to master the skills being taught.

4. *Student progress is controlled by their own competence.* Application of this characteristic prevents student time and motivation from being wasted by requiring more advanced students to mark time while others catch up. It also means slower students won't have to shortchange themselves on practice to catch up.

5. *Instruction is directly related to accomplishment of the objectives.* Therefore, most or all instruction time will be devoted to teaching what needs to be learned.

6. *Instructional materials impose a minimum of obstacles between the learners and the learning.* Thus, unnecessary impediments to learning are avoided.

7. *Instruction is presented through the simplest delivery mechanisms consistent with the objectives, the learners, and the learning environment.* This saves time and money by ensuring that students will get the instruction they need through the simplest and most direct media that will do the job.

8. *Students are provided with an opportunity to practice each objective and to obtain feedback regarding the quality of their performance.* Learning is more effective when students practice what they are learning, and when they receive immediate information about how well they are doing.

9. *Learners receive repeated practice in skills that are used often or are difficult to learn.* Application of this characteristic ensures that difficult-to-learn and often-used skills will receive periodic refreshment during a course.

10. *Learners receive immediate feedback regarding the quality of their test performance.* This allows a test procedure also to be a learning experience, which is positive and useful. It will also avoid the problems caused by delayed feedback.

11. *Desired student performances are followed by consequences they consider favorable to them.* Because people learn to avoid punishing experiences, this practice will

ensure that motivation is strengthened rather than weakened.

12. *Within the limits imposed by content and equipment constraints, learners are free to sequence their own instruction.* Therefore students will, within the limits imposed by content and equipment, spend their time studying something in which they are currently interested.

13. *The learning environment itself contains the facilities and equipment needed to implement the above characteristics.* This way neither you nor the student will waste time, get frustrated, or miss important things because of missing items or the need to retrieve items from remote locations (such as regional AV centers).

14. *Students will learn how to recognize correct and incorrect performance before being allowed to practice the skill to be learned.* This means that students will learn what is needed to make their practice sessions productive.

It is seldom possible to put all of these and other ideal characteristics into practice. There are, after all, time constraints, money constraints, and space and equipment constraints, to name a few. Therefore, course procedures are rules that will implement the ideal as closely as possible. In plain language, we derive course procedures that will allow us to say, "I am teaching absolutely as well as constraints will allow."

## HOW TO DO IT

Review the ideal characteristics listed above. These characteristics were derived from what we know about how to make learning happen effectively and efficiently. In other words, instruction that has these characteristics will be about as good as we presently know how to make it.

Now, for each of the characteristics listed, ask yourself the following questions:

1. Can you implement the characteristic as stated?
2. If so, write the rule that will tell students what to do.

3. If not, why not? What prevents you from implementing the characteristic?
4. Can you think of a way to get around that constraint?
5. If so, take the action needed to get around the constraint, and then write the rule that will put the ideal characteristic into practice.
6. If not, can you think of a way to get around the constraint even a little bit? In other words, can you think of a way to reduce the obstacle to implementing the characteristic?
7. Take the action needed and then write the rule or rules that will come as close to implementing the characteristic as is possible.

**Example:** One of the ideal characteristics of instruction is "Student progress is controlled by their own competence." This means that the most efficient instruction is that which allows students to progress to something new as soon as they have learned what they are working on now. It means that students are not forced to begin new material before they have mastered the old and that they are encouraged to progress to new material as soon as they have mastered the old. (Sometimes students will develop the skill called for by an objective before they develop confidence in their ability to apply the skill. When this happens, they will often ask if they can practice a little more before moving on. If you can, provide the practice. At other times you will find that students are so delighted with their new skill that they want to exercise it— fondle it—some before moving on. When this happens, they are literally enjoying the subject matter. Unless time presses, it is good to allow this to happen. It helps student confidence or motivation, or both.)

To show you how to think through the questions above, I'll put some sample "thinking" in the form of a monologue. That way you can see what goes on in the head of someone deriving course procedures.

1. We are considering the characteristic "Student progress is controlled by their own competence." Can you implement the characteristic as stated?
   *No way.*

2. Write the rules.
      *Not applicable.*
3. What prevents you from implementing this characteristic?
      *This school has always had a 50-minute hour, and instructors are expected to have all students progress at the same rate.*
4. Can you think of a way to get around that constraint?
      *Well, I suppose I could ask for a policy change, but it seems unlikely it would happen in my lifetime.*
5. If so, take the action needed to get around the constraint.
      *Can't think of a way around this constraint.*
6. If not, can you think of a way to get around the constraint even a little bit?
      *Well, I could simply make some changes within my own class without even needing any change in policy. I could give the students the course objectives and the course materials and ask them to tell me when they are ready to demonstrate their skill. When they can perform OK, I could then let them go on to the next objective.*
7. Take the action needed and then write the rule or rules that will come as close to implementing the characteristic as is possible.
      **Course Procedures:** *When you think you have accomplished an objective, you may ask for the test. If you can perform according to the standards (criteria), you may move ahead to the next objective.*

Let me offer a suggestion at this point. Whenever you find yourself saying, "I can't do it" or "It's against school policy," look a little closer. Many of these "policies" have never been written down, and many of them aren't real. They are only things that everyone believes. Question them.

Another thought. There are many things that you can do differently without ever having to ask for anyone's blessing or approval. After all, you're being paid to exercise your best judgment to get the job done. If you go to your administration or to your management for approval of every change you want to make, you'll soon earn a reputation for being unable to do anything on your own. So think about it. If you can change the color of the paper on which your tests are printed without requiring anyone else's approval, you can change the rules by which you operate your course. And if you *can* change some of your practices without demanding approval, you can come closer to implementing ideal instruction just by deciding to do it.

## A SIMPLER WAY

Here is a simpler way to derive course procedures. Use the model set of procedures listed below as your guide. It is a set of procedures used by those who are in a position to implement most or all ideal characteristics. Just imagine that this will be the set of procedures by which you will implement your course. Where you see a procedure that you cannot implement, only then do you need to answer the questions above and make changes.

The closer you can come to following these procedures, the closer you will be to applying what is known about making instruction work.

---

**Model Course Procedures**

Following are the procedures or rules by which this course is conducted. In general, the procedures tell you to select the module you want to study, to proceed at your own rate, to ask for the Performance Check when you are ready to do so, to work with others as much or as little as you wish, and to use as few or as many resources as you feel you need or want.

### How to Begin

1. Read these Course Procedures.
2. Be sure you know the location of the resources, the Performance Checks, the Self-Evaluation material, and the Master Progress Plotter (the sheet that shows the modules completed by each student in the course).

3. Begin with Module _____ . It is a short introductory unit that will show you the big picture and provide you with a mental map of where you are heading.
4. Use only the resources (readings, practice material) you feel you need to help you develop the skill defined by the objective of the module.
5. Practice the skill at least once before asking for the Performance Check.
6. Take time to muse, talk to others, and to see how others are applying the skills they are learning. This is not a race. Use the opportunity to sharpen your skills.

## Course Map

The Course Map shows how each module of the course is related to other modules and to the course as a whole.

1. Before beginning to study *any* module complete *all* the prerequisites for that module (i.e., all modules shown by lines and arrows to lead into that module).
2. The location of a module on the map represents a suggestion as to the approximate point in the course where it will be most meaningful to you. Where no sequence is shown (i.e., where there are no arrows leading into a module), feel free to study those modules in any order you wish.
3. Place an "X" or some other mark on those modules the instructor indicates are optional for you.

## Modules

1. Before beginning a new module series, read the introductory comments at the front of the module booklet. The diagram facing the introduction shows how the modules in that booklet relate to the rest of the course.
2. Study only one module at a time, but feel free to put that module down and study another that you are eligible to enter whenever you wish.
3. Begin a module by reading the Objective and the description of the Performance Check (or sample test item).
4. When you feel qualified to do so, ask the instructor for the Performance Check. (It's a good idea, however, to read

through the entire module so that there won't be any terminology surprises.)
5. Work through the module at your own speed.
6. If you are not sure of your competence, complete all the practice exercises. If you are still not sure, check with the instructor.
7. The instructor will provide a signup sheet for those modules that include group practice. Sign up for the session most convenient for you.

## Resources

1. There are at least three resources for each module: the module itself, other students, and the instructor. Additional resources may also be available. If so, they are listed on the first page of the module.
2. Consult any of the resources you think may help you, but do not feel compelled to consult them all.
3. When resources are listed in a module, the relevant page numbers are indicated. Feel free to read more widely if you wish, but keep the module objective in mind as you do.
4. Feel free to ask other students which resources they found most helpful; provide the same information for others if they ask.
5. Work with a colleague whenever you wish.

## Performance Checks (Criterion Tests)

1. Ask for a Performance Check whenever you feel ready. Before doing so, however, you will save time if you first make sure you can answer "yes" to these questions:
   a. Did I practice the skill called for by the objective?
   b. Did I get a colleague sign-off, if it is called for by the module?
2. If, after reading a module, you feel ready for the Performance Check without further study, go for it.
3. Take only *one* copy of the Performance Check.
4. If you do not perform adequately on a Check, you may, after further study or practice, complete the same Check again, or a similar one, at the instructor's discretion.

5. When you have completed a Performance Check, ask for the Self-Evaluation material and check your work. The instructor or whoever is qualified to do so will then check your work.

### Personal Progress Summary

Ask whoever is checking your work to date and initial your Personal Progress Summary next to the appropriate module. This is your verification that you have been checked off on that module and are free to move to another.

### Master Progress Plotter

When your Personal Progress Summary has been initialed for a module, make sure the instructor makes the proper entry on the Master Progress Plotter. That will be your indication that your progress has been recorded.

## OPTIONAL COURSE PROCEDURES

You may find a need to write other course procedures, depending on the nature and location of your course, the amount of equipment available, and the time available. Here are some examples:

- Complete all the modules below the line shown on the Course Map before working on those above it.
- When you have completed all the modules below the solid line shown on your Course Map, you will be eligible for the group practice session. Sign up for it at that time.
- When a module asks you to complete a practice exercise, write directly on the worksheets supplied in your module booklets.
- Resources may be checked out overnight. Sign them out, and remove your name when you return the resource.
- Be sure to read the instructions before using the videotape recorder.
- You will find equipment to practice on in Room _____ . This room will be open from 10 A.M. – noon, and from 3 P.M. – 5 P.M.

- When you enter the practice room, take a tag from the door and replace it when you leave. This will tell other students how many pieces of practice equipment are available at any given time.
- If the work you have completed for a Performance Check is not yet adequate, and if the instructor had to revise or modify it, it will be considered the instructor's work and you will be asked to repeat the Performance Check after some additional practice.

- If, at any time during the course, you feel that there is too much reading, you are probably doing one or more of the following:

  — Working alone instead of with a colleague when a module suggests it.
  — Plodding through a resource you consider uninteresting or inappropriate for you instead of putting it down and finding another.
  — Using printed materials as your primary source of information instead of relying on colleagues and the course manager as well.
  — Spending too long with a problem before asking for assistance.
  — Working through *all* the resources listed in a module, instead of using only those required to develop the desired skill.

**To Learn More:** See Resource #17.

# 19 | Implementing the Instruction

**Situation:** *Everything has been prepared, and students are about to arrive.*

Implementation means delivering the instruction to the students. Naturally, you want to do the best job possible. How can you make sure that you do just that?

## SUCCESS

Recently I questioned several instructors individually about their vision of instructional success. I asked each of them, "What would things look like if your instruction were totally successful?" In other words, what would be the result if everything went as you wanted it to? Though they used different words in their replies, the contents were quite similar. Here is a summary of how these instructors visualize instructional success.

1. Students leave the instruction having accomplished the objectives set out for them.
2. They are eager to apply what they learned.
3. They are eager to learn more.
4. They can speak coherently about what they have learned.

In other words, successful instruction sends students away who can do, are willing to do, and who have a favorable attitude toward the subject. Does that coincide with your own image of instructional success? If so, it clearly implies that *how* you teach can be at least as important as *what* you teach. This is because a favorable attitude toward a subject—a willingness to talk about it and an eagerness to use what was learned and to learn more—is shaped in large part by the actions of the instructor. For example, an instructor who demeans or belittles students when they attempt to demonstrate their skill will find those students backing away from the subject.

## CONSEQUENCES

Because instructor behavior is so critical to successful instruction, you must pay careful attention to how you behave in the presence of your students. Whether you like it or not, *you* are an instrument of reward and punishment, an instrument that will cause students either to want to learn more of your subject or to want to hear no more about it. Whether you like it or not, your own behavior shapes the attitudes of your students. For example, consider the effects of the following instructor statements:

> "Look. This is a dumb film, but I'm supposed to show
> it and you're supposed to watch it."
> "I already answered that question three weeks ago."
> "If *that's* the best you can do, maybe you should be in
> some other department."
> "Don't try to get ahead of the class."
> "This class isn't as sharp as the one I had *last* year."

And if you think back over your own history as a student, you'll be able to think of dozens of other examples of instructor behaviors that served only to turn students off. The sad thing is that these behaviors occurred mostly because the instructors were unaware of what they were doing or unaware of the effects of what they were doing. Fortunately, there is a way to avoid the accidental turn-offs and to maximize the deliberate turn-ons. Here's how.

1. *Learn to identify desired student performances.* You cannot increase the probability of desired performance if you don't know what that performance is. Or, in plain language, you gotta know what you want, to get what you want. So take a few minutes to make a list of the things you consider to be productive (desired) student performances. Answer the question, What things do I want my students to do while learning? Here's a start on your list.
   - Ask questions when something is not clear.
   - Ask for additional practice material.
   - Practice the skills to be learned.
   - Offer to help other students.
   - Keep trying until they can perform as desired.
   - Spend time maintaining their tools.
   -
   -

2. *Learn to identify the favorable consequences at your disposal.* If you smile on undesired performance, you may get more of it. If you offer the equivalent of a pat on the back when a student is goofing off, you may get more of that, too. If you frown, however, or somehow insult or demean a student for asking questions or for trying, you'll get less of those positive efforts. So make a list of the things you might do in response to desired performance. And if you're thinking, "There's nothing I can do," you've never been more wrong. You ought to be able to list at least two dozen things that you could do to encourage desired performance when you see it. I'll help get your list started.
   - a smile
   - a pat on the back
   - a favorable comment
   - a little extra attention
   - a little time off (even a few minutes works)
   -
   -

3. *Check your performance.* The easiest and most private way to find out whether you are encouraging desired performance

and discouraging undesired performance is to set up a video camera in the back of the classroom or lab and just let it record. (Don't tell me you don't have such equipment available to you. If your institution doesn't have it, which is hard to believe, then you have a friend who will lend you one.)

Review the tape in private. Look for examples of desired student performance, and then watch to see what you did in response. Did you ignore it? Did you punish it? Or did you pay attention to it, smile on it, say something nice about it? This simple review will show you how you might modify your own performance so that you will get more of what you want and less of what you don't want. Your goal should be to "glow" on desired (productive) performances and to ignore unproductive performances wherever possible.

## PEOPLE SEE, PEOPLE DO

Instructors who tell students to do something one way and then do it (model) another will find their students becoming inattentive to their words. Instructors who demonstrate apathy or indifference to what they are teaching will soon find their students doing the same. Instructors who model enthusiasm for their subject and for learning, however, will often find these characteristics rubbing off onto their students.

Few truths have been as well established by research as the fact that most of what we learn during our lives is learned by imitation. We see things done and we try to do likewise. We read about how things are done, our instructors show and tell how they are done, and we try to do likewise. To paraphrase Dr. Albert Bandura, if we learned mainly by trial and error, the world population would be a lot smaller than it is; a lot fewer of us would survive adolescence.

Because modeling is such a powerful instructor, it is imperative to instructional success that you do as you want others to do, that you act as you want your students to act, lest you accidentally reduce their interest in the subject you are teaching and motivation toward learning. Here is a summary of the main modeling principles and an example to illustrate the application of each:

1. Observers learn by watching and imitating others; they tend to behave as they have seen others behave.

    *Application example:* If you want students to observe certain safety precautions, then *you* observe them—especially when you are in their presence.
2. Observers will be more likely to imitate a model who has prestige in their eyes.

    *Application example:* Have desired performance demonstrated by someone your students respect: a manager, local hero, football player, rock star. If you have prestige in the eyes of your students, it is doubly important for you to practice what you preach.
3. Observers will be more likely to imitate modeled performance when they see the model being rewarded for that performance.

    *Application example:* When one student performs to expectations, make sure you respond positively to that performance (e.g., with a smile, favorable comment, token).
4. Observers who see a model being punished will be less likely to imitate the performance that was punished.

    *Application example:* If a student is punished (demeaned, insulted, ridiculed) for attempting a difficult task and making a mistake, other students will be less likely to attempt the difficult task themselves.

Unhappily, you may not be able to tell when you are accidentally putting students down. (I recall an excellent instructor who took all questions seriously. But while he thought about an answer, he would scowl and tug at an eyebrow, which intimidated other students and made them reluctant to ask their own questions.) Fortunately, there is a simple solution. Put a TV camera in the back of your classroom and let it record as you teach. At your convenience you can review the tape while pretending to be a student. You will easily be able to spot the opportunities for improvement.

## CONDUCTING THE COURSE

There are two main formats in which instruction is implemented:

1. Instructor-controlled (instructor-led), and
2. Performance-controlled.

### Instructor-Controlled Instruction

This format has been traditional for hundreds of years. In this format the instructor is the primary source of information, which is usually offered to students mainly as lectures (presentations). The main advantage is that a single instructor can present information to as many students as can be brought within eye- and earshot, which, through the use of television, can amount to millions.

The main disadvantages are that individual attention is very difficult to arrange, all students must receive the same instruction in the same way and at the same pace, and students cannot practice individually for as long as they need to become proficient.

### Performance-Controlled Instruction

In this format the students' progress is controlled by their performance. Only when they have mastered one objective are they encouraged to move to the next. Though this format can accommodate a number of instructor-led presentations as well as group sessions when called for by the objectives, it is usually conducted in a self-paced mode.

Self-pacing means that students learn and practice for as long as they need (within limits) or want. It means that when they can demonstrate that they have met the criteria established for accomplishment of one objective, they may move to the next. It does *not* mean that students do as they please or that there is a lack of discipline (unless "discipline" is defined as lack of student mobility and activity). It also does not mean that there is an absence of instructors.

The advantages of this format are that (a) each student has the opportunity to successfully accomplish all of the objectives,

(b) students have some control over the sequence in which they address the modules, (c) instructors can devote most of their time to coaching individual students, and (d) all principles of learning can be applied toward effective learning. Another large advantage is that the instruction can be guaranteed to accomplish the objectives that analysis has revealed as important.

Disadvantages are that instructors require some coaching before they can manage this format and that some instructors find it difficult or impossible to handle this type of outcome-oriented structure (they would much rather perform than coach). Another "disadvantage" is that lead time is required to prepare the materials. Though this is also true of the instructor-led format, instructors have so often been expected to "wing it" that many people have *erroneously* come to believe that good instructor-led instruction takes little or no preparation while a performance-based course takes enormous preparation time.

> **NOTE:** There is a distinction that you should insist on making when discussing these instructional formats. Performance-based (criterion-referenced) instruction has been designed to accomplish specified objectives, whether or not that instruction is delivered in an instructor-controlled or performance-controlled format. This distinction is easy to remember if you think of it this way. All instruction should be designed to fill a need; that is, all instruction should be designed to accomplish important objectives. But once prepared, that instruction can be delivered in different ways: it can be delivered through instructor-controlled or performance-controlled formats.

## PRESENTATIONS

No matter what the format of your instruction, you will always have occasion to present information by means of the lecture. When this is the case, you are acting as a transmitter, a broadcaster, of information, and your own behavior is critical. For example, if students cannot easily understand your words, all your preparation and all your expertise will be of little value. So if your diction is poor, or your accent so heavy as to be difficult to understand, you yourself become an obstacle to learning. In such a case you should clean up your speech or get out of the classroom.

There are other characteristics that a good presenter (lecturer) should have if he or she is to facilitate learning rather than interfere with it. Here is a list. The effective presenter

1. speaks clearly and understandably,
2. has mastery of the subject matter,
3. models desired student performance,
4. models enthusiasm for the subject and for learning,
5. provides positive consequences for desired performance,
6. can operate instructional equipment,
7. uses visuals in timely manner and without causing distraction,
8. diagnoses individual student problems and recommends remedies, and
9. can handle a variety of instructional methods (e.g., discussions, question-and-answer sessions, role-plays).

## HOW TO DO IT

Whether you are experienced or inexperienced, your presentations will benefit from periodic checkups. Because we are prone to picking up distracting mannerisms . . . er . . . ah . . . and gestures over time, the wise instructor periodically reviews his or her presentation behavior at least twice a year. This is done by following one or both of the following procedures:

1. Videotape one of your presentations, and then pretend you're a student and review it in private as you answer the checklist questions (found on the next page).
2. Give your students a copy of the checklist and ask each of them to complete it at the end of one of your presentations.

Since the instructor is the key instrument through which instruction is offered in the instructor-led format, it is important that that instrument be kept in fine tune.

## PRESENTATION CHECKLIST

| | Yes | No | ? |
|---|---|---|---|
| 1. Was the objective of the session clear to you? | | | |
| 2. Was it clear *why* the content or skill is important to *you?* | | | |
| 3. Did the body of the presentation seem organized from your point of view? | | | |
| 4. Were you "taught" things you already knew? That is, was there more content than was needed to learn the objective? | | | |
| 5. Did you have opportunities to ask questions? | | | |
| 6. Did you get helpful answers to those questions? | | | |
| 7. Did you have an opportunity to practice what you were taught? | | | |
| 8. Was your practice followed by prompt and useful feedback? | | | |
| 9. Was the instructor easy to understand? | | | |
| 10. Did the instructor seem interested in what was being taught? | | | |
| 11. Did the instructor do anything to belittle, insult, or demean you or other students? | | | |
| 12. Did the instructor have any distracting mannerisms? If so, what were they? | | | |
| 13. Did you accomplish the objective of the lesson (module)? That is, can you now perform as the objective describes? | | | |

## MANAGING THE
## PERFORMANCE-CONTROLLED COURSE

In this format the instructor functions more as a coach than as a performer. Though the instructor is encouraged to instruct where necessary, the main burden of the instruction is carried by other media, such as audiotape, videotape, videodisc, print (manuals, texts, booklets), simulators, or computer. The instructor provides resources, diagnoses student problems, instructs when necessary, and verifies performance progress. Though the course may be self-paced, it is not conducted without an instructor (unless it is designed to be a self-study course). In fact, this format asserts that instructor time is too valuable to be wasted on matters that can be better handled through other means.

Instructors using this format have a great deal more control over learning progress than those using the instructor-led mode. When students have to demonstrate an ability to perform on one objective before they are encouraged to move to another, the instructor can have constant and instant knowledge of where each student is in relation to course completion and can take immediate steps to make corrections when needed.

If you have occasion to conduct a criterion-referenced, self-paced course, you will need to think of yourself as a coach or consultant rather than as the main dispenser of information. This means that you will spend most of your time assisting individual students: diagnosing their difficulties and recommending corrective action, providing additional practice opportunities, reviewing performance and offering feedback, and reinforcing (glowing on) student successes and partial successes.

In addition to the skills listed earlier for classroom presenters, you will need only to develop your coaching skill to the point where you can sit with an individual student and calmly provide the answers to questions, demonstrate a procedure, and review performance. Because you will be closer to the student than when you are standing in front of a classroom, you will need to modify your gestures; sweeping gestures are fine when you are lecturing but inappropriate when working with individuals. You don't want to run the risk of knocking their glasses off or giving them a bloody nose while you are making a point.

For the same reason, you will want to make sure you don't create other obstacles to learning as, for example, would be the case if you had bad breath. (I can no longer use course managers who are smokers in our criterion-referenced workshops, since more than 90 percent of our attendees are now nonsmokers and try to avoid sitting close to those who smell of stale tobacco.)

## HOW TO DO IT

When you are ready to conduct the performance-based course in a self-paced manner, here are the steps to follow:

1. Begin with an orientation session. Explain to students what the course will be about, and hand out a copy of the objectives. Answer questions about the objectives so that everyone knows what they will be expected to be able to do to be considered competent.
2. Hand out a copy of the course procedures and make sure everyone understands the rules by which you will be operating. They won't believe you at first no matter what you tell them, so you will have to repeat this information from time to time, and you will have to be sure to live up to the procedures yourself.
3. Make sure students know where to locate all the resources, and explain the items uppermost in their minds at this time (i.e., what are the hours, where's the bathroom, and what about breaks).
4. Tell them how to begin the course. Make sure they each have a copy of the course map, and explain the constraints and the options. Make sure everyone understands any symbols or conventions you have used in drawing the map, and make sure they understand what to do as soon as you end the orientation session.

5. As soon as the orientation session is over, wander around from student to student and remind them again where and how to begin. This may be the first time they have been given an opportunity to have anything to say about their own learning, so give them time to adjust. It will take a day or two, after which there will be no stopping them.
6. Follow the course procedures.


**To Learn More:**   See Resource #8.

# PART

# IV

# Improving the Course

# 20 || Course Improvement

Situation: *You want to locate opportunities for improving your existing instruction and to make those changes that will give the most benefit for the least effort.*

A course is *effective* to the degree that it accomplishes what it sets out to accomplish. It is *efficient* to the degree it accomplishes its purpose with the least motion (time, effort, money). Since nothing is perfect, everything can be improved, including instruction. But just because instruction *can* be improved is not enough reason to go to expensive lengths to do so. If the instruction is doing what it is supposed to do, if it is doing so without undue cost, and if it is sending students away with more rather than less interest in the subject, it should be considered successful. Although you should make improvements when the need or opportunity arises and you should make efforts to detect opportunities for improvement, a constant (and usually expensive) hunt for *perfection* is not a cost-effective use of your time.

Having said that, let's consider course improvement. This is something you do all the time. You do it when you refine your lesson plans, you do it when you make equipment more readily available to your students, you do it when you solicit opinions about the course, and you do it when you make the instruction more tightly related to the objectives.

## IMPROVEMENT REQUIRES CHANGE

Though it is always necessary to change something in order to improve it, the reverse is not true: change doesn't always mean improvement. To improve something means to make one or more of its characteristics come closer to some ideal or desired state. But you can say that improvements have been made only if you know what you are trying to achieve, if you know the objectives you are trying to accomplish. For example, if you can say, "Hey there, I gave a thirty-minute talk today and only said 'aah . . . ' twelve times compared to yesterday's leventy-seven times," *and* if aah-less speech is the goal, standard, or ideal you are trying to achieve, *then* you can say that you have made an improvement.

Think of it this way. Improvement is the last of a four-step process.

1. **Measurement.** The first step is measurement. When you determine the extent of some characteristic, you are measuring. For example, "It's six feet long" is a statement about a measurement.
2. **Evaluation.** When you make a judgment based on a comparison of a measurement with a standard, you are evaluating. For example, "It's too short" is a statement of judgment. The thing measured has been compared against a standard or ideal and found not to match. If you have no standard against which to compare a measurement, you cannot tell whether the thing measured is OK or not OK.
3. **Opportunities for improvement.** When you locate discrepancies between measurements and standards or ideals, you identify opportunities for improvement. For example, "Five percent of my students didn't accomplish all their objectives during the time allotted, but they *all* should have," means that the comparison of the percent completing and the *desired* percent completing showed a difference, or discrepancy. It also means that a possible area for improvement has been identified.
4. **Improvement.** Improvement is the action taken to cause one or more characteristics to move closer to the ideal or desired condition. For example, "I increased the amount of practice time, and now only 1 percent of my students don't accomplish all the objectives in the time available" means that action has been taken to successfully reduce the difference between what exists and what is desired.

## WHAT SHOULD I MEASURE?

Depends on what you want to know. With all the statistical techniques that are available, it would be possible to collect mountains of numbers about a course. But most of them would be worthless. Why? Simply because most of that information would be of no use in making practical improvements. Most of it would simply amount to counting angels on the head of a pin. So relax. Course improvement is relatively easy if you keep your eye on the possible.

As I said, what you measure is determined by what you want to know. So what *do* you want to know about your course? As soon as you decide what you want to know, you will know what to measure. There are three main things you should want to know about your course.

1. **Does it work?** That is, is it effective? Does it do what it is supposed to do?
2. **Is it of value?** That is, does it fill a need, either of the student or of the institution or organization?
3. **Is it efficient?** That is, is it up to date? Does it match the state of the art? Does it impose minimum obstacles between the student and the learning?

## WHEN TO DO IT

The first two questions (Does it work? and Is it of value?) should be answered at the end of the course. The third question should be answered continually throughout the course.

## HOW TO DO IT

Figure 20.1 will help you to visualize the method for answering the three key questions. Read the graphic like this. We start in the "real world"—from a real need, whether that be to teach someone to perform a job, to be prepared for the next course(s), or to function more successfully in some type of community. Through the analysis procedures we derive the objectives of the instruction. We then develop instruction intended to accomplish those objectives. Through the instruction we develop competent students and then send them off to that portion of the world for which we have prepared them.

**Figure 20.1**

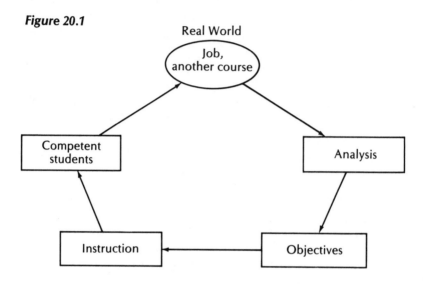

Now here's how to think about answering the three key questions.

1. **Does it work?** This question is answered by comparing student performance with the objectives of the instruction. It is not answered by looking at the content of the instruction, at the instructional procedures, or at what people are doing on the job. (By now you know that there are several factors that influence what people actually do on a job, or in a classroom, and that skill is only one of them. In other words, there are many reasons why people may not do what they know how to do. That's why it is not possible to assess whether training works by watching their "real-world" performance.)

For example, if 95 percent of the students accomplished the objectives, then the course is "working" for 95 percent of the students. If 100 percent is the desired number, then there is an opportunity for improvement of 5 percent.

**Figure 20.2**

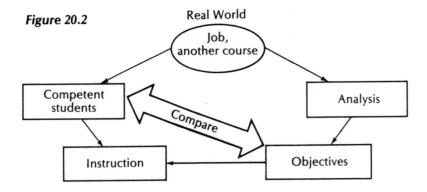

2. **Is it of value?** This question is answered by comparing the objectives of the instruction with the needs that gave rise to them. In other words, this question is answered by verifying the accuracy of the analysis that led to the objectives, by comparing the objectives with the need. It is not answered by looking at the content of the instruction or at the instructional procedures. If students no longer need to be able to do some of the things taught in the course or need to learn things not currently taught, then the opportunity for improvement lies in readjusting the objectives to meet the current need.

Thus, the question, Does it work? is answered by determining whether the instruction does what it *sets out to do,* and the question, Is it of value? is answered by determining whether the instruction sets out to do something that *needs doing.*

**Figure 20.3**

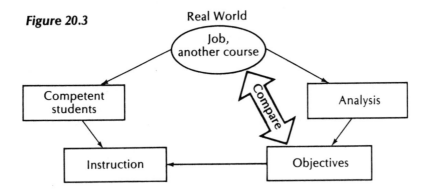

3. **Is it efficient?** This question is answered by comparing the instructional practices against the state of the art (expressed in terms of ideal characteristics), that is, by determining how closely those practices match the ideal characteristics. For example, if you noted that your tests did not yet match your objectives (for whatever reason), then you would have noted a discrepancy between what you *had* and what you *could* have had if your tests matched the state of the art, and you would have identified an opportunity for improvement. For another example, if you noted that students were not yet allowed to progress on the basis of their competence, you would have noted a discrepancy between what you were doing and what you should ideally have been able to do and identified another opportunity for improvement.

**Figure 20.4**

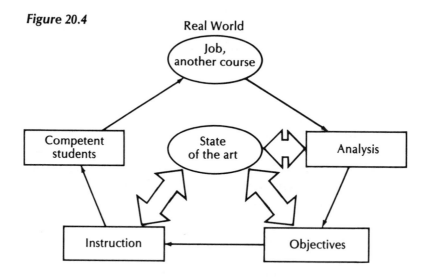

Here is a checklist of some questions that will help you spot opportunities for improvement. You can derive your own list by reviewing the ideal characteristics presented in Chapter 18 and preparing questions that will allow you to determine just how well the course currently implements each of them.

# A COURSE IMPROVEMENT CHECKLIST

A checkmark in any but the Yes column represents an opportunity for improvement.

## Objectives

|  | Yes | No | ? |
|---|---|---|---|
| 1. Do you have objectives for your course, stated in performance terms? | | | |
| 2. Are the objectives derived from the job, craft, or vocation being taught? | | | |
| 3. If your students feed into another course, are your objectives derived in part from the prerequisites of that course? | | | |

## Course Materials

|  | Yes | No | ? |
|---|---|---|---|
| 1. Does each student have a copy of the course objectives? | | | |
| 2. Is the instructional content confined to what is needed to accomplish the objectives (i.e., includes no irrelevant instruction)? | | | |
| 3. Are the instructional materials all keyed into the objectives so that students know which materials are relevant to the accomplishment of each objective? | | | |
| 4. Are the materials understandable to the students? (Ask them.) | | | |
| 5. Are the instructional materials readily available to students in the learning environment? | | | |

## Course Procedures

| | Yes | No | ? |
|---|---|---|---|
| 1. Does each student have a copy of the course procedures? | | | |
| 2. Do students report that these procedures are actually followed? | | | |
| 3. Do students have a course map or similar document showing how all the skills of the course relate to one another? | | | |
| 4. Do course procedures pose a minimum of obstacles between students and the learning (i.e., do course procedures facilitate rather than hinder learning)? | | | |
| 5. Are trainees free to move around the learning environment (subject to safety restrictions and group-related restrictions dictated by course objectives)? | | | |
| 6. Do students have immediate access to course components such as texts, manuals, equipment, parts, diagrams, videotapes? | | | |
| 7. Is the environment free of avoidable distractions such as noise, interruptions, discomfort, harsh or low lighting, uncomfortable temperature? | | | |

## Practice

| | Yes | No | ? |
|---|---|---|---|
| 1. Does each learner practice each key skill? | | | |
| 2. Is immediate feedback available for practice exercises? | | | |
| 3. Can each student practice until the objective has been accomplished? | | | |
| 4. Is at least half the instruction time devoted to practice? | | | |

## Instructors

| | Yes | No | ? |
|---|---|---|---|
| 1. Have you had training in | | | |
| a. classroom presentation skills? If not, have you taken steps to assure that your presentations match the characteristics of the Presentation Checklist on page 175? | | | |
| b. instructional development? If not, will you promise to make the improvements suggested by this Checklist? | | | |
| 2. Do you model the performance you expect of your students; i.e., do you practice what you preach? (Ask the students.) | | | |
| 3. Do you behave positively toward students rather than belittle or insult them? (Ask the students.) | | | |
| 4. Do you behave positively toward the subject you are teaching; i.e., model enthusiasm? (Ask the students.) | | | |
| 5. Are you proud of students' growing competence? Do you show it? (Ask the students.) | | | |
| 6. Do you make yourself available to assist individual students during the learning session? | | | |

## Students

| | Yes | No | ? |
|---|---|---|---|
| 1. Do students exhibit a strong desire to learn what you are teaching? | | | |
| 2. Are students encouraged to practice only those skills in which they need improvement? | | | |
| 3. Are students allowed some choice in the sequencing of their study? | | | |
| 4. Are students allowed some choice in the method of learning and in the instructional resources they use? | | | |
| 5. Are students allowed to practice until they have accomplished an objective? | | | |
| 6. Do students receive individual attention when they need it? | | | |
| 7. Are students encouraged to move to another unit of instruction when their competence has been demonstrated on the present one? | | | |
| 8. Does something desirable happen from the students' point of view when they reach competence in all the objectives (e.g., favorable comments, cheers, applause, diploma, time off)? | | | |

## Performance Tests

|  | Yes | No | ? |
|---|---|---|---|
| 1. Are students encouraged to demonstrate their competence (take the performance test for the unit they are studying) when they feel ready to do so? |  |  |  |
| 2. Does every test item measure a course skill (i.e., does each item match the objective it is measuring in terms of performance and conditions)? |  |  |  |
| 3. Do students receive immediate and constructive feedback on their test performance? |  |  |  |
| 4. When a student's performance is judged to be not yet competent, is the weakness diagnosed and additional assistance given—without belittling the student? |  |  |  |
| 5. Is the student required to demonstrate competence in each key skill before being considered competent in the skills being taught? |  |  |  |

## OPPORTUNITIES KNOCKING

Once you've spotted some opportunities, you'll want some guidelines for sorting them out. It's one thing to spot an opportunity for improvement; it's something else to decide whether the improvement is worth making. Sometimes an improvement would cost far more than it is worth. For example, suppose you find a way to shorten a course by 10 percent. That would be worth thinking about doing, especially if the shorter course would be just as effective. But suppose the cost of that potential improvement is far more than you or your organization can afford? The thing to do is to keep the possible improvement in mind against the day it can be made in a more cost-effective manner.

For another example, suppose you note that you could make the course work a lot better (improve the effectiveness) by letting students work for 4-hour stretches over 5 consecutive days rather than for 50 minutes 3 times each week for X weeks. And suppose you also know that you'd have about as much chance of changing local policy as a goose has running a marathon on a pogo stick. What to do? Look for other opportunities. Here's a way to think about the priority for taking advantage of the opportunities.

## Attack Rules

1. *Quick Fixes.* Make the easiest changes first, regardless of the payoff. For example, if you spot a dozen opportunities for improvement, and the easiest to implement would be to make your overheads more readable, do that first, even though it may add only a little to the effectiveness of your instruction. Making the easiest fixes first will get you moving and will give you some fast successes about which to feel good.
2. *Independent Fixes.* Make the changes that don't require the assistance or approval of someone else, regardless of payoff. If you can improve the course a little bit today, that's at least as good as improving it a lot next year. For example, if you could make your tests match your objectives without needing approval to do so, that would be a higher priority change than that of trying to get approval to teach your course in a single 40-hour block.
3. *High Payoff Fixes.* Make the fixes that will provide the highest payoff in course effectiveness, even if approval is required. Here is the list of actions that will give you the most return for your efforts, in order of priority.
   a. *Make objectives match the need.* Check your objectives against the need from which they were derived to make sure that they reflect what students need to be able to do. The highest priority way to make instruction work better is to ensure that the objectives are worth teaching.
   b. *Provide outcome information to students.* If you do nothing else, make sure that a copy of the objectives is in the hands of the students. This act will give them a fighting chance to accomplish the things you want them

to accomplish, even though instructional materials may be scarce or poorly crafted.

c. *Provide a reason to learn.* Once students know what is expected of them, the next best thing to do is to make sure they have a solid reason to learn. So make those changes that will help students to perceive how it is important to *them* to accomplish the objectives: make sure the need is clear, make sure students can practice when ready, make sure they find out how well they are progressing, and make sure you have eliminated as many obstacles to learning as you possibly can. And remember that "Someday this will be important to you" is not a reason to learn. Instead, it is a symptom of instruction that hasn't yet been made relevant to the students.

d. *Provide instructional resources.* Give the students whatever materials and other resources are currently available, regardless of their quality. When students *want* to learn, they'll do it in spite of inadequate resources.

e. *Provide a supportive environment.* Once the above steps have been attended to, the best way to improve the quality and efficiency of your instruction is to improve the learning environment itself.

- Provide easy access to resources. Make sure that as many resources are available in the classroom itself as possible and that access isn't restricted by unnecessary bureaucratic rules.
- Minimize obstacles such as distractions, whether these are provided by noise, students, instructors, or outsiders.
- Make sure students know it's OK to practice and perform as desired and that it's OK to make mistakes while learning.
- Be available to help, but stay out of their way.
- Offer positive consequences for desired performance, as well as for *approximations* toward desired performance.

f. *Adopt more streamlined procedures.* Go back to your course procedures and see where you can modify them to more closely approximate the ideal instructional characteristics found in Chapter 18.

g. *Improve the instruction itself.* Polish the presentations, hone the examples, and clarify the visuals. It may come as a surprise that this item is on the bottom of the priority list. But think about it a moment. What good is it to improve the elegance of the instruction itself if that instruction serves no useful purpose, or if everyone is convinced that it is of little or no value to them? How much will it add to the effectiveness or efficiency of a racing car to paint it when the tires are flat and the engine is dead? Sure, it's important to improve the elegance of the instruction itself: smooth instruction helps motivation as well as ease of learning. But until the above items are attended to, improved elegance isn't likely to net you much gain in instructional success.

So work to make the course responsive to a real need before working to improve the elegance of the course materials. Work to provide students with a real reason to learn before working to improve the quality of your slides. Remember Wacky Watchmaker who worked hard to reduce the number of parts needed for a wristwatch. When asked whether it worked, he replied, "Certainly not. But it doesn't work—*efficiently*."

And keep in mind that Rome wasn't burned in a day. Make your changes one at a time. And then reward yourself each time you do so.

## IN CLOSING

Vocational and technical instruction is an act of humanity. It is the attempt to enrich the lives of others by expanding their ability to deal more successfully with the world in which they live. The measure of our success is the degree to which we can make our graduates employable, self-sufficient, and socially adept.

There are few callings more personally rewarding or of greater importance to society than that of contributing to the success of others.

# Resource List

## Resource

## Available from:

1. Mager, R. F., and Pipe, P. *Analyzing Performance Problems.* 2nd ed., 1984.
2. Mager, R. F. *Developing Attitude Toward Learning.* 2nd ed., 1984.
3. Mager, R. F. *Goal Analysis.* 2nd ed., 1984.
4. Mager, R. F. *Measuring Instructional Results.* 2nd ed., 1984.
5. Mager, R. F. *Preparing Instructional Objectives.* 2nd ed., 1984.
6. Pipe, P. *Objectives: Tool for Change.* 1975.

Lake Publishing Company
500 Harbor Boulevard
Belmont, CA 94002
    (Phone: 415-592-7810)
(Resources #1– #6)

7. Performance Analysis Worksheets (24/pkg.).
8. Mager, E. W. *Classroom Presentation Skills Workshop.* 1985.
9. Mager, R. F. *Applied CRI.* 1987.
10. Mager, R. F., and Pipe, P. *Criterion-Referenced Instruction: Analysis, Design, and Implementation.* 2nd ed., 1982.
11. Mager, R. F. *Instructional Module Development.* 2nd ed., 1984.

Center for Effective
    Performance, Inc.
4250 Perimeter Park South
Atlanta, GA 30341
    (Phone: 404–934–5859)
(Resources # 7-#11)

12. Carlisle, K. E. *Analyzing Jobs and Tasks.* 1986.

Educational Technology Publications, Inc.
140 Sylvan Avenue
Englewood Cliffs, NJ 07632.

13. Cram, D. D. *Professor T-Pop.* Performance and Instruction, July, 1979, pp. 38–41.

14. Cram, D. D. *Advice to the Training-Lorn.* Performance and Instruction, March, 1983, pp. 26–27.

15. Hoffman, M. *What to Leave Out When Time Is Short,* Performance and Instruction, April, 1987.

16. Harless, J. H. *Guiding Performance with Job Aids,* Introduction to Performance Technology, 1986, pp. 106–124.

17. Tosti, D. T. *Feedback Systems,* Introduction to Performance Technology, 1986, pp. 166–167.

National Society for Performance and Instruction
1126 Sixteenth Street NW
Washington, DC 20036.
(Resources #13–#17)

18. Pipe, P. *Developing Performance Aids.* Peter Pipe Associates, 1981.

Peter Pipe Associates,
962 Chehalis Drive
Sunnyvale, CA 94087

# Makenzie Mit Der Bookentesting

The houselights dimmed and the orchestra charged into the overture. Cymbals crashed, trombones trombled and trumpets hootled. Violin bows flashed and bobbled in unison, as though locked together in a frenzy of musical calisthenics.

"That's a pretty enthusiastic overture," said the novice. "What's this opera about, anyway?"

"Well," responded the regular, "it's a tribute."

"Tribute? To what or whom?"

"To a clump of folks who were generous enough to help the hero test his book. The opera opens with the hero sitting at the typewriter, writing a book. He begins by singing and whining about how hard it is to write. It's a very sad aria."

"Sounds like a nut. What happens then?"

"His wife comes in . . . Hildegard Lollapalooza. She's a soprano played by Eileen Mager. She tells him about her day in the village. Then they sing a duet, with her trying to get him to let her see the book, and him subtly trying to get back to work."

At this point the first act ended and the smokers ran for the exits.

"What happens next?" asked the novice.

"The next act takes place after he's finished a first draft and is ready to try it out."

"Try it out?"

"Yes. Before he sends it to the publisher he wants to know whether the book has the right content for its audience, and whether it's as clear and useful as he can make it."

"Isn't he smart enough to answer that for himself?"

"Well," replied the seasoned one, "He's smart enough to know that his mind-reading skills aren't very good. So to make sure he's headed in a useful direction he's asked someone to check it for continuity and completeness."

"Aha."

"Here he comes now. The first person to run his mind over the manuscript is Doctor Magic Whizzmore, played by Paul Whitmore." Just then a dashing figure in flowing robes entered and began to sing in sonorous tones.

"Why is he carrying that box under his arm?"

"That's his computer. He always carries it. Shhh. Listen as he tells the writer about his findings, about his reactions to the content. It's a very moving song."

"Now what?"

The soprano had returned and repeated her aria entreating the writer to let her see his work. He bends down to tie his shoelace; while on his knees he begs the question.

"The suggested revisions have now been made and another tryout has been done, this time by the baritone in the purple knickers waving the golf club. This role is being consummately played by David Cram . . . he plays it often. He's singing about how he checked the manuscript for completeness and content, as well as for its integrity in the corporate training environment."

"Does he always carry that golf club?" queried the novice.

"He has to. It's attached to him. His doctor has told him that if he ever unscrews the golf club from his hand, his bottom will fall off."

"This seems like a long opera."

"They all do. The music covers the absence of plot, and the loud singing helps keep the audience awake. But we're nearing the climax. Look. Here come the Teepoppers."

"The what?"

"The Teepoppers. They represent the primary audience for the book. The writer has asked people with a great deal of experience in vocational and technical schools to check the manuscript for content, clarity, and appropriateness in that environment. They're singing their recommendations. These roles are brilliantly played by Bob Miller and Jim Maxey. This is important stuff. Notice how closely the writer is paying attention and making notes."

"Wait a minnit. Here comes that soprano again. What does she want now?"

"Same thing. Wants to offer her help, but the husband keeps telling her he's saving her for the grand finale. Even so, she's good for his morale."

"How does it come out in the end?"

"Wait and see. Look. Another round of revision has been completed and the writer has sent out copies for technical accuracy."

"I thought he just did that."

"That was to make sure the content would work for the audiences it is intended for. This check was to make sure that the content and procedures are psychologically sound and accurately apply known principles of learning."

"Looks like a parade is starting."

"No. It's just that each of the people asked to check technical accuracy sings a recommendations solo in turn. Gives us a chance to see some colorful costumes as we listen to their wisdom."

"Who are playing these roles?"

"These roles are incomparably played by Marianne Hoffman, Bill Valen, Carol Valen, and Paul Whitmore."

At this point the soprano returned and the curtain came down on the second act.

"The last act opens with the chorus singing about the title check," confided the veteran. "The writer has asked a number of people to respond to several possible titles. They sing about their choices while the writer sings about the importance of making the title fit the intended user."

"I've just become glad they don't sing this stuff in English."

"If you will think about it you will see that this is a very important part of the process. How often would you buy a steak that was called dead cow?"

"I see your point. Who are these people?"

"These roles are ably played by Al Wilson, Carol Valen, Lex Danson, John Pate, Skip Wolfe, Millar Farewell, Seth

Leibler, Joyce Kelly, Verne Niner, Bill Valen, Alan Steffes, and Eileen Mager."

"The soprano finally got a whack at it?"

"Yes. And now she's into her big scene. She was saved for last, y'know. Loved ones can be the hardest critics and he didn't want to take a chance on being demoralized before he finished. But she finally got to do her manuscript tryout and is now singing her recommendations."

"Long, isn't it?"

"But beautifully sung."

"Why is that lady in the black mask and red cape slashing at the manuscript?"

"That's the editor, played by Barbara Armentrout. She's the heavy, acting out how she sliced words and punctured phrases to ready the manuscript for publication."

"Couldn't he write?"

"No matter how well he writes there are always hundreds of changes that will make the thing more readable, more literate. Also gives editors a feeling of power.

"Look. Here's the grand finale. The writer has assembled all the contributors into his den. . . . "

"Big den."

"Artistic license. He's describing their important contributions to the development of the book and is singing the praises of each in turn. He's imploring the audience to stand in awe at their assistance and to applaud their generosity until their hands turn red. Let's join in."

And so they did.